My Love Affair With...
POLITICS & PARTIES

Family & Political Life in Rhode Island and New York

*For Annette —
one of the few good friends I've
made in Palm Beach.
Love,
Isabelle*

My Love Affair With...

POLITICS & PARTIES

Family & Political Life in Rhode Island and New York

ISABELLE RUSSEK LEEDS

American Life Publishers

Boynton Beach, Florida

American Life Publishers, LLC
Boynton Beach, FL 33472
(561) 254-1883
www.americanlifepublishers.com

© 2008 by Isabelle Russek Leeds
All rights reserved, including rights of reproduction. No part of this book may be used or reproduced in any manner without the written permission of the publisher, except in the case of brief quotations embodied in critical articles or reviews.

Published 2008 by American Life Publishers

ISBN 978-0-9791086-1-7

Library of Congress Control Number 2008924531

Unless otherwise noted, all photographs, illustrations, and memorabilia in this book were taken from the Isabelle Russek Leeds family collection. The publisher extends special thanks to the photographers who generously granted permission to reprint specific photos for this book.

Jacket Design by Adrienne Panico and Patricia Mavo
Book Design by Adrienne Panico and Mike Herbert

Printed in the United States of America

*This book is dedicated to my father
who made it all possible
and to my children
and my grandchildren
who made it all so full of joy*

You must give some time to your fellow man.
Even if it's a little thing;
do something for those who have need of a man's help,
something for which you get no pay but privilege of doing it.

-Albert Schweitzer

TABLE OF CONTENTS

Foreword — ix
Preface — xi

1. Rose & Lou and the Founding of Standard Romper (Health-tex) — 1
2. Growing Up — 12
3. Wellesley College — 26
4. Family Life in Rhode Island — 35
5. Rhode Island Politics, 1950s - 1960s — 50
6. "I Love New York"
   Political Life in New York City, 1970s - 1995 — 74
7. WMCA Radio — 102
8. Alternate United States Representative to the United Nations — 104
9. Palm Beach and Retirement — 109
10. Social Gatherings and Philanthropy — 114
11. Good Friends — 128
12. Reflections — 135

FOREWORD

I am proud to have been asked to write a forward to Isabelle's wonderful memoir. Let me begin by saying that after sixty years and thousands of hours of conversations, I thought there could be nothing new for me to discover about my dearest friend. After all, I have followed every step of her career as a political pioneer and watched with admiration as she made an impact in every endeavor she ever undertook whether political, organizational, or charitable.

From our early beginning as college roommates, I have watched people gather around her and always marveled at how effortlessly Isabelle attracted and maintained friends spanning all generations and from every walk of life. Of course, I could not help but see how she also enjoys fashion and her delight in both giving and attending parties. Perhaps most significant of all is that she has never allowed her work to interfere with her devotion to her children and grandchildren. In this book, we see Isabelle in her totality, and she is even more remarkable. This is a very human story of a woman who had the courage and the conviction to begin a new chapter on women in American politics.

Lorraine Silberthau
Former Press Secretary to Rhode Island Governors
Frank Licht and J. Joseph Garrahy

PREFACE

I often think about the wonderful life I have led, one that has spanned eight decades, during a momentous time in our country's history and indeed, that of the world. I have had many fulfilling moments over the course of eighty-one years, as well as many challenging ones. Sharing these experiences with loved ones was my primary motivation for writing this personal history. Since I know little about my forebears, I wanted you, my children and my grandchildren, to have a better understanding of your heritage and of the events that have shaped us as a family and as individuals.

The writing of this book has been a long, but rewarding journey, and there are a number of people I wish to thank for supporting me through its development. First, I would like to extend my gratitude to Patricia Mavo, without whose guidance and patience this project would never have come to fruition. Her encouragement, editorial wisdom, and historical perspective have been invaluable along the way. I must also thank Ira Neimark, whose enthusiasm for his autobiography led me to undertake my own. I am very grateful to Alvin Chereskin and Arthur Hurvitz for their contributions to the Health-tex chapter. Without their valuable input, I would not have been able to fully reconstruct the story of my father's company.

Special thanks go to my dear friend, Lorraine Silberthau. She and I have been friends for sixty years and during all that time, I don't think more than sixty days have passed in which we did not speak. We were roommates in college, bridesmaids in each other's weddings, and colleagues in the world of politics. After I moved to Providence, Lorraine's home town, our relationship deepened through our mutual political involvement. The depth of our trust for each other and our ease in exchanging confidences has made my friendship with Lorraine one of the most meaningful relationships of my life. She possesses superb judgment and has a wonderful facility with words. This combination led two generations of political leaders to seek her services, so it's not surprising that I sought her talents as well. She was extraordinarily helpful. Finally, I would like to thank my children for their suggestions. This book is for them and I am pleased that they were able to participate in its creation.

It was my desire as well that this work offer some historical perspective. Over the years, I have met and worked with many dedicated and talented people, and I have been fortunate to partake in political and social worlds that few Americans ever experience. The rewards of political life are many, and I would encourage any young person who reads this book to consider a life in public service.

KNIT GOODS
STANDARD
CENTRAL

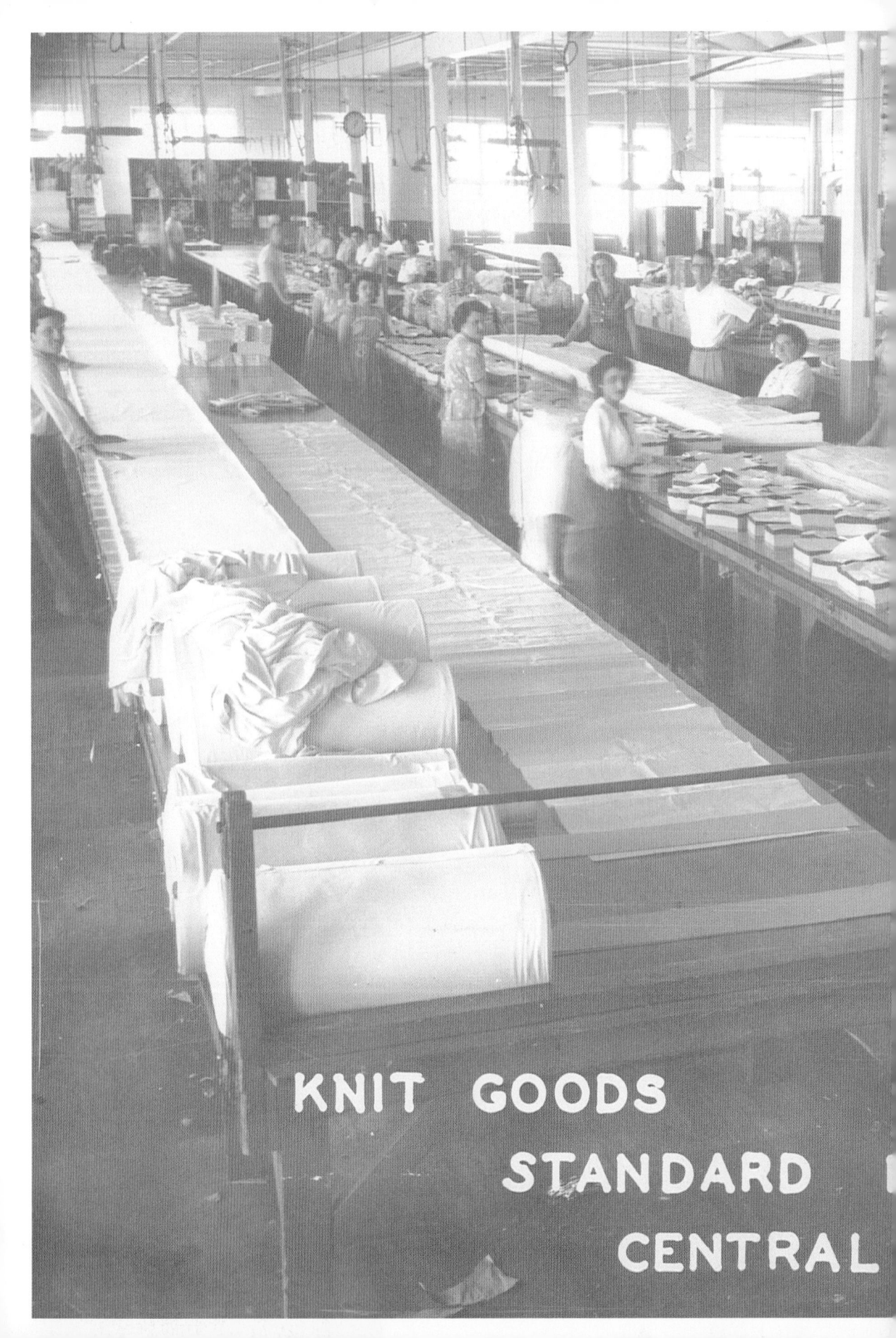

ROSE & LOU AND THE FOUNDING OF STANDARD ROMPER (Health-tex)

1

*I*n the late nineteenth century, along with thousands of other immigrants, David Russack and Becky Aginsky Russack left their home in Russia for a new life in the United States. With them were their four children: Herman, Ida, Anne, and Mary. When they arrived, the processing officials asked for the children's birth records and like many immigrants of the time, my grandparents had none to present, so all of the children were assigned the same birthday of September 15th. After settling in New York, Becky gave birth to two more children, my father Louis, followed by his sister Rose. Every year, the siblings celebrated all of their birthdays on that same September day.

David opened a newsstand in Harlem, a Jewish neighborhood at the time, and after he saved enough money, he bought an apartment house on upper Park Avenue where he and Becky raised their family. With the outbreak of World War I, my father joined the Army and as his troop's ship crossed the Atlantic Ocean, it was torpedoed. Fortunately, Lou and the rest of the crew were rescued and his troop went on to serve in France. On that same ship was another young man from New York City, Joe Love. He and my father became good friends and remained so their entire lives. Later, they both rose to prominence as two of the most innovative and successful entrepreneurs in the children's clothing industry.

2 Rose and Lou and the Founding of Standard Romper (Health-tex)

Soldier Louis Russack, World War I

Near the time that my father's parents left Russia, Hyman Bauman and Minnie Brown also emigrated from Russia and settled in the town of Burlington, Vermont. A Talmudic scholar, Harry translated the Torah into English for Burlington, and he and Minnie raised their family of four: Moe, Esther, my mother, Rose, and Abe.

Sometime around 1920, Rose left Burlington for a life in New York City. By then, Lou had returned from France and was working for the Manchester Romper Company. My father's entrance into the world of soft goods took place while doing a good deed.

After his military service, Lou returned to New York and went job hunting. As he was walking down the street one day, he saw a truck driver harassing an older Jewish driver. Still in uniform, Lou walked over and intervened. The grateful man then offered Lou a ride and asked, "What are you doing now that you're out of the Army?" "Looking for a job," Lou replied. "Well," said the older man, "I have a small clothing business called Manchester Romper Company and I'd like to offer you a job as a salesman." Thus began my father's career as the premier childrenswear manufacturer in the country. Also working at Manchester Romper was an inside man, Morse Gould. Lou and Moe developed a good rapport and decided to start their own business. In 1921, they founded the Standard Romper Company, later known as Health-tex.

Meanwhile, Rose had found a job as a cashier in a restaurant Lou happened to frequent. One day, Lou walked into the restaurant and when he saw my mother, he said, "I'm going to marry you," which he did in 1921—the same year that he and Moe founded Standard Romper. Rose became pregnant with twins, but tragically, both died at birth because the doctor delivering them was drunk. A few years later, I was born in 1926, followed by my sister Norma in 1929.

Rose and Lou
and the Founding of Standard Romper (Health-tex)

After Lou and Moe established Standard Romper, the company grew fairly quickly. Much of its success has been credited to my father's charisma, honesty, and his remarkable skills as a salesman. Standard Romper produced a line of childrenswear under the Stantogs label and sold its creepers and rompers to small apparel stores in the Northeast. As its popularity grew, the company expanded its markets across the country. Then in 1937, the Health-tex label was introduced to emphasize the "healthy" cotton and wool fabrics that the company used to manufacture its playclothes. The Health-tex brand became a household name as the company marketed directly to consumers through advertisements in women's magazines. By 1960, Health-tex was the country's most popular childrenswear brand. It produced it own knitted fabric and each season introduced a new line of clothing created by in-house designers.

The popularity of Health-tex clothes was due in large part to the quality of the material the company used. As former president, Arthur Hurvitz, recalled, "Mothers used to write to us and say that the Health-tex clothes were so durable and long-lasting that they were able to pass them down from one child to the next." In fact, it was Arthur's father, Morris Hurvitz, of M. Hurvitz & Company, who provided Health-tex with its quality knit textiles. Lou Russack (later changed to Russek) wanted the best for his childrenswear and Morris Hurvitz supplied him with sturdy knits that handled well during manufacturing and performed equally well on active children. Health-tex placed such a demand on M. Hurvitz's production capabilities that Morris decided to accept Lou's offer to merge his company with Standard Romper. The companies merged in January of 1944, and Morris joined Lou's team as executive vice president. They moved the company's New York-based manufacturing business up to Central Falls, Rhode Island, and later expanded with plants in Maine, Alabama, and Virginia. Health-tex also opened showrooms in Chicago, Dallas, Los Angeles, and San Francisco.

*Seated left to right: Louis Russek, Chairman of the Board
Arthur Hurvitz, President
Standing left to right: W. T. Samiljan, Vice President of Sales
Alvin Fields, Vice President of Merchandising
Leon Gould, Vice President and Secretary
Nat Regen, Vice President of Finance-Treasurer (© 1973 Health-tex Inc.)*

When Standard Romper began to think about increasing its national advertising, Lou met with Alvin Chereskin, the head of AC&R Advertising. My father's reputation preceded him and the company he led was well-respected as described in this letter to me from Alvin:

Health-tex distribution center, Rhode Island (© 1973 Health-tex Inc.)

Inside one of the Health-tex plants (© 1973 Health-tex Inc.)

> *Health-tex was looking for an advertising agency . . . we met, obviously liked each other and quickly won the business. We immediately knew we would be dealing with a strong presence and savvy personality in Mr. Russek . . . All the research and talk with the industry media*

Rose and Lou
and the Founding of Standard Romper (Health-tex)

and retail executives conveyed a great respect for Health-tex... [it] had the unique reputation for being a most profitable and desirable brand to carry... This was a company whose mission was to give the public a product with inherent integrity in its pricing, practical styling design, and lasting wearability... Mr. Russek also gave the small retailer as much attention as he did the giant retailers. During World War II, it was the small ma and pa operations that were loyal to his company when the larger department stores were not... So our job as an agency was not to sell more product... but to help the brand [overcome its reputation] as a basement name... Although the Health-tex brand used better fabrics and had more detailing, it did not have the prestige and fashion appeal for the carriage trade... This brand was as good as the other choices they had available upstairs. Mr. Russek was the first one to make sure that infants never had to have their tops put over their heads... He put buttons on every knit top, [which] was copied by every other brand. (Alvin Chereskin, 2007)

Lou and Alvin launched their advertising campaign called the "Handy answers to hard questions asked by children in the Health-tex years," which featured colorful print ads that provided answers to the types of questions asked by children, such as Why do I have to drink milk? Why do we dream? Why are people different colors? The ads were illustrated by

Alvin Chereskin and Isabelle

Susan Perl and featured children dressed in Health-tex clothes along with a postscript reminding customers of the versatility and durability of Health-tex apparel. The ads first ran in the *New York Times Magazine* and met with instant success, particularly with mothers and teachers who pasted the ads on their refrigerators or in their classrooms. Letters poured in and the *New York Times* sent out a special mailing about the company to hundreds of advertising agencies and retailers from Neiman Marcus to Macy's. The ads were later combined to produce three children's books which sold very well. It was always a thrill for my family to walk into a friend's home and see the ads on the refrigerator, something I am told happened all over America.

Walt Disney then asked Susie to develop a vehicle using Health-tex children as the basis for a children's cartoon series, but neither my father nor Susie would agree. Nor would my father agree to license Health-tex kids as soft dolls or produce Health-tex shoes or sneakers. Lou was a great merchant and entrepreneur, but he did not want to license the company name. While he may have seen the value of franchising, he felt that he would have no control over the quality of the merchandise produced, so he would not consider that method of expansion. A lost opportunity, I believe.

In 1971, the company went public and the Standard Romper Company officially changed its name to Health-tex. In a newspaper interview that year, Lou described the company he founded and his commitment to the small-store owner despite the prevailing emphasis on big accounts and big orders:

> *We've got more than 7,000 accounts on our books and we have a great respect for the small merchant. I believe that there is plenty of room for that kind of merchant, and I become more convinced of it when I observe the warm interest of the small store owner in his customer in contrast with the impersonal and often neglected attitude that the customer meets in the large store . . . We've survived fifty years with our kind of operation. ("A Friend of the Small Retailer," New York Times, November 7, 1971)*

Rose and Lou and the Founding of Standard Romper (Health-tex)

Lou was always concerned with the integrity of his product and preferred to sell to small and middle market department stores rather than the large discount stores. Eventually, the Health-tex brand became so popular that the company had difficulty meeting demand and was forced to institute an allocations program. "We had to allocate how much each regular customer could buy from us in order to control quality," explained Arthur Hurvitz. "It took six months to train a sewing operator, and if Health-tex expanded too rapidly, quality would be compromised."

In 1973, the company was acquired by Chesebrough-Pond's and new plants were added that helped ease the allocation restrictions. Health-tex then changed ownership in the late 1980s and was later bought by the VF Corporation in 1991. VF made the decision to remove the hyphen in the company's name after finding that consumers sometimes associated Health-tex with a healthcare firm. Today, Healthtex is a division of the New York-based children's apparel manufacturer, LT Apparel Group, formerly known as Lollytogs.

Over the years, many of our family members worked at Health-tex. My uncle, Alex Kourland, was a member of the firm and at one time both my husband, Marshall Leeds, and my sister's first husband, Al Fields, held management positions. My father's brother-in-law, Murray Steckler, and my mother's brother, Abe Bauman, worked in the Rhode Island plant. Also in the business were my cousins, Irwin Kourland, and George and Harold Gemeiner, who were star salesmen. Although it may only be family lore, the story is that since Harold wore the same size shoe as Lou, he would break in every new pair that Father bought.

Going public, New York Stock Exchange. Left to right: NYSE President Robert Haack, Louis Russek, and Arthur Hurvitz. (printed with permission of Wagner Photos)

Morse Gould and Louis Russek receiving a 25th anniversary plaque from their employees, Providence, RI, 1946

Early on, I had asked my father if I could join the company, but at the time my husband was working there and he didn't think it was a good idea. Instead, I became involved in politics. After I moved back to New York from Providence, however, I once again expressed a desire to work for the company and submitted a sample series of marketing materials called the "Health-tex Herald," which could be distributed at the point of sale. By then, Health-tex was a public corporation and some of the new executives vetoed the idea. I would like to think that if I had been given the opportunity, I would have helped to advance the company, although I certainly never regretted the career path my life took instead. After my father retired from the board of Chesebrough-Ponds, I suggested to Ralph Ward, the chairman of the corporation, that I might fill his position on the board. He gave short shrift to that idea.

Lou Russek devoted enormous energy to his business and the company prospered. The workers in his factories were treated so well that year after year they voted against establishing a union. Eventually, the decision was made to call in the union, but in the many years that followed, business and labor always enjoyed a warm relationship under my father's

Rose and Lou
and the Founding of Standard Romper (Health-tex)

leadership. At one time, the employees at the company's Central Falls plant presented a plaque to Lou and the management team in tribute to the plant's excellent industrial relations.

As a child, and indeed throughout my entire life, I was very close to my father. Although he devoted so much time to Standard Romper, he always found time for his family. My sister and I always called him Father, never using the more familiar word Daddy. I looked up to him, respected him, and I guess, idolized him. I am very much like him—tall, independent, a perfectionist, often cranky and hypercritical—although I hope my family and friends find that I am pretty nice underneath it all. There is no question in my mind that he was the major influence in my life. Not only did his genius provide me with the wherewithal to live a life of luxury and ease, but he gave me the philosophy of my life—to be generous and loyal to family and friends, to give something in return for the plenty in my life, to respect the rights of others, and to treat all people alike. It was his insistence on integrity that prompted what I hope is my own. He was reserved and appeared rather severe, never a hail fellow well met, and I

With my father

Louis Russek (Photo by Bachrach)

Standard Romper

think of myself that way. Father was stern and I think a lot of people were afraid of him, but he was also very kind and generous. Not only did he support many members of his family, but during World War II, he always made very large, anonymous contributions to the war effort, as well as to many local and national charities. Watching his example helped me to develop a strong sense of what John F. Kennedy once said, "From those to whom much has been given, much is expected." I was always proud to be Louis Russek's daughter and I think, and hope, that I earned his pride.

GROWING UP
2

This photo was always on my mother's dresser

When I was very young, we lived in New York City. What I remember most about those days was that because of the kidnapping of the Lindbergh baby, my mother would not allow us go outside to play on Thursday, the maid's day off. "That's the day when the kidnappers are out" she would warn us. I also recall winning a spelling bee in the second grade. When I was six or seven, I contracted the chicken pox, which traveled to my eyes. I sat in bed with my eyes bandaged for three days. When the bandages finally came off, I began wearing glasses and did so until contact lenses first became available while I was in college. Those early lenses were large, thick, and required a plunger to remove.

Before I entered the third grade, we moved to 21 Earlwood Drive in White Plains, New York. Norma and I attended Post Road Elementary School and then White Plains High School. A chauffeur took us to school every day, and I was so embarrassed that I would always ride in the front (a habit I still have) and would often get out of the car before we reached the school to avoid being noticed. Although my mother wanted to send me to Fieldston (a private school in Riverdale, New York), I refused to go. I loved my school and part of the reason I resisted changing was probably related to the crushes I had on several of the football players. It was also during this time that my father had our name legally changed from Russack to Russek after becoming increasingly irritated with teachers and staff who kept pronouncing our name as Roosak. I seem to remember some of our relatives saying that Russek had been the original spelling anyway.

At age eight, I realized that most of the girls in my class had a middle name, so I said to my mother, "Everyone I know has a middle name, and I want one also." Then my sister chimed in, "Me too!" "All right," my mother replied, pointing first to Norma. "You are my Joy," and to me she said, "You are my Sunshine." Immediately I realized that Sunshine was not the kind of name I had in mind, and I insisted, "No, I

Growing Up

want to be Joy!" "Okay," said my mother, "That is how it will be." So, I became Isabelle Joy and my sister was saddled with Norma Sunshine.

A year or two later, I complained that we were the only family on the block without a Christmas tree. I must have carried on quite a bit because after we went to bed on Christmas Eve, my father went downtown, bought a tree, and decorated it with loads of ornaments. When I came downstairs Christmas morning, it was the happiest day of my life, although my parents were embarrassed to have any relatives visit until the tree came down. It seems that I insisted on my own way from an early age.

Growing up, we had nine newspapers in the house. The *New York Times* and the *Herald Tribune* were delivered in the morning, the *White Plains Reporter Dispatch* arrived around 4:00 p.m., and a bit later, the *New York Post*. Each evening the chauffeur would go the station and pick up the early editions

Isabelle & Norma

of the *Daily News* and the *New York Mirror*. When my father came home at night, he had the *New York Journal American*, the *New York Sun* and the *World Telegram* tucked under his arm. At his office, he read the *Wall Street Journal* and one of the trade papers. When I went off to college, I had a hard time deciding which papers to have and decided on the *Times*, the *Post*, and the *Journal*. New York's afternoon daily papers have disappeared, and now I read only the *Times* and the *Post*, the first for news and the latter for gossip.

Growing Up

During our childhood years, my mother employed a wonderful couple named Birdie and Lee Becker. Birdie was a world-class cook and housekeeper, and Lee was a great driver and all-around handyman. I believe they loved my sister and me as if we were their own and we cherished them too. Birdie's favorite expression was "sweet peaches," a saying that my daughter Amy lovingly recalls to this day. Birdie and Lee were with my parents until they retired, shortly before my mother's death. They were the sweetest, kindest, most competent people in the world, with the exception only of Celia and Manuel Fraga, the wonderful couple who look after me in Greenwich, Connecticut. I am also fortunate to have an excellent couple, Neuemia and Manuel Neto, who take very good care of me in New York and Florida.

It was while the family was living on Earlwood Drive that for the first and almost the only time in my life I encountered overt antisemitism. Between our driveway and that of the next-door neighbor's, there was a thin concrete slab, perhaps three or four inches wide. My sister and I used to walk up and down that divider, occasionally losing our balance and falling off to one side or another. Whenever we fell on the neighbor's side, someone would come running out and shout, "Get away from here. Why don't you go back to where you belong?" Eventually, our neighbors overcame their antisemitism and their daughter, Marian Pierce, and I became good friends and were bridesmaids in each other's weddings. Also, when my children were born, the maiden aunt of that family presented me with a ceramic piggy bank inscribed with each baby's name, gifts that Amy and David continue to keep on display. Earlwood Drive remained our family's home until my mother died in 1967.

Near the time that we moved to White Plains, Rose, my father's youngest sister, and her husband, Alex Kourland, moved to 37 Riverside Drive with their two children, Irwin and Lorraine. The two families were very close, and Lorraine and I were the dearest friends. I was always jealous that she lived in the city and I had to be in White Plains. I remember my mother and Aunt Rose sitting for hours in the bedroom overlooking Riverside Drive, gossiping, while Lorraine and I, and sometimes Norma, listened intently to every word that they spoke.

Among some of my favorite childhood memories were visiting my grandparents every Friday night and the family seder celebrations each year at Passover. On Friday nights, my grandmother would prepare a Sabbath meal of chicken soup, roast chicken, potatoes and vegetables with fruit for dessert, accompanied by my favorite cookies known as "keichel," something like the Italian biscotti. At Passover, the Russeks and the Kourlands would go to my grandparents' home and in later years, to my Aunt Annie Agadstein's where my grandfather, and subsequently, my father and my Uncle Alex, would conduct our ever shorter seders. Each year, the highlight was the final singing of Had Gadya. We always had a wonderful raucous time. As a girl, I occasionally accompanied my father and grandfather to services at the orthodox synagogue. To this day, I relive that experience each Yom Kippur when in spite of my membership and regular holiday attendance at the Reform Temple Emanuel, I attend Yizkor (memorial) services at Park East Synagogue, an orthodox institution on the Upper East Side of New York City. The reason I go there is that the Ark is dedicated to my mother.

As children, the Russeks and the Kourlands vacationed together at our summer cottages in Mount Tremper in the Catskill Mountains of New York—the village consisted of only two buildings: a post

Aunt Rose, Cousin Lorraine, and Uncle Alex Kourland

Growing Up

office and a general store. Our homes adjoined farmland where a herd of cows usually grazed. One of our favorite summertime occupations was throwing corn cobs over the fence and watching them eat our leftovers. I also recall walking into a hornets' nest and being bandaged from head to toe. In those days, you were allowed to have your own fireworks, and every Fourth of July my father and Uncle Alex would put on a shower of different displays. Then one summer, we had to be evacuated from our home via horse and wagon when the small creek across from our cottage overflowed. Although I did not dine out on stories at the time, I must say that we were provided with plenty of composition material for years to come.

The story of the flooded creek leads me to a more recent experience that took place in Florida. On a day in 2006, Palm Beach received an historic amount of rain. I was having lunch at the country club with my friend, Barbara Rackoff, and since she did not have her car, she asked if I could drive her home. As we turned into her street, I noticed that the water on the road was becoming rather deep. There was a driveway close by that was higher, so I attempted to turn into it. At that moment, my motor flooded, the electrical system shut down, and we were stuck. We couldn't open the doors or windows, so we used our cell phones to call for help. Both the police and fire departments told us that since there were so many cars stuck, they couldn't get to us for awhile. About then, a large truck drove by creating a wave of water that covered the car, and with that, the water started to rise inside. Barbara and I thought that was the end and we started screaming. All of a sudden, something else happened to the electrical system and the front seat started moving forward and pushing me into the steering wheel. Frantically I tried to open the door and there must have been an angel on the fender because the door opened and we scrambled out. We plowed through water that was well over our knees, finally reaching Barbara's house where we both scurried to take off our wet clothes, jump into a shower, and try to regain our composure. I borrowed Barbara's robe (she is five feet tall) and the sight of me (at just under six feet) in her robe was pretty comical. After many calls, we succeeded in reaching the doorman at our country club who agreed to come and pick me up. His only condition was that I meet him at the corner since the street was too flooded for him to drive through. So again I plowed through the water and soon arrived home to once again strip off wet clothes and take a hot bath. I also needed a stiff drink. Unlike the flooded creek story of my childhood, I did dine out on this tale for months, but it was far more traumatic than my earlier experience. Incidentally, my brand new Lexus was totaled.

At the age of thirteen, I fell in a hole and developed water on the knee, which had to be tapped the next day. That procedure was one of the most painful episodes of my life. Two years later, I developed a loose cartilage in that same knee and had the first of many surgeries. In those days, the need for physical rehabilitation was not widely recognized, and I did not receive the proper physical therapy. As a result, I have had a lifelong series of problems with my right knee.

My mother also had knee surgery at one point which was probably linked to the rheumatoid arthritis that would sometimes send her to bed for days. Although she had a life of material comfort, she suffered great physical discomfort. The doctors thought that it would be good for her to get out of the cold winter weather, so off we went to Miami Beach. The twenty-six hour train ride to Miami was always a lot of fun for Norma and me. We loved going to the dining car, eating southern fried chicken, and wrapping up the evening with bingo and a horse racing game in the lounge car. It was in Miami that I was introduced to what is still my favorite dessert, cocoanut layer cake. Whenever I misbehaved, my worst punishment was not being allowed to have my beloved sweet that night.

Growing Up

We attended the Lear School on Collins Avenue and 17th Street. Classes were held right on the beach and were limited to five to seven students, and we could see and hear the ocean waves as we studied. When we returned to White Plains, I was so far ahead of the other students that I skipped a grade. We went back the following year and the same thing occurred. That is how I happened to graduate from high school at the age of sixteen and college at twenty. Although those were the only two years we stayed the entire winter in Miami Beach, we continued to spend the Christmas holidays there for many years to come, staying first at the Atlantis Hotel and then at the Roney Plaza. During World War II, the Army Air Corps was stationed in Miami Beach, and they used to parade daily up and down the boardwalk outside of the Roney. Clear in my memory is the sight of the singer Tony Martin among the

marchers. Some years later, when Dean Martin and Jerry Lewis were appearing in Miami Beach, the nightclub where they had been performing had a serious fire. Since they were staying at the Roney Plaza, they came to the pool every afternoon and put on a show for the guests. They were hysterical and from that time forward, I followed their career with great interest.

When the Fontainebleau Hotel was built, my parents switched their allegiance to the newer hotel, and I would occasionally visit them there for a few days. Then in the early 1950s, my parents discovered the Whitehall in Palm Beach and that became our vacation destination. Once we started vacationing in Palm Beach, my only association with Miami Beach was visiting my cousin Lorraine who had moved there in the 1980s. I would accompany her and her husband, Sidney Cooperman, to dinner at Joe's Stone Crabs, which had been a favorite restaurant of mine. One year, when my son David was about fourteen, my father took us there along with his friend, Georgie Jessel (then a famous comedian) and his girlfriend. David was so busy staring at the beautiful, buxom showgirl friend of Jessel's that he hardly ate a mouthful.

Despite the pain she suffered, my mother was a very kind person who loved people, loved to play cards, and loved to entertain. My sister was very much like her—very pretty, very sweet, and much softer than my father and I. Although she loved to entertain, my mother did not cook very much. While she may have done so as a young bride, the only

My mother Rose

things I remember her making were cheesecake and gefilte fish. Evidently, they were so delicious that all her friends clamored for a few pieces. As far as I was concerned (and still am), the fish is only as good as the horseradish that is heaped upon it. The

Growing Up

infrequency of my mother's trips to the kitchen is one of the few characteristics I seem to have inherited from her.

Although I loved my mother very much, she did not really understand me. I believe she thought that I had delusions of grandeur, which may have been true to some degree. Years later, I had a long

One of my favorite photos of Father

discussion with Bess Myerson (a former Miss America and a woman of great beauty and intellect) about how Jewish mothers of that generation treated their strong, independent daughters. Our consensus was that they expected us to be perfect and since we did not live up to their standards of perfection, the mothers became hypercritical. I can remember being a teenager, ready for my first evening gown, and my mother was incapacitated, so my father took me shopping. We came home with a long, white pleated gown. I was so excited to try it on for her, but when she saw me she said, "You look just like a bottle of milk in that dress." Needless to say, I never wore it, and in fact, it was nearly fifty years before I bought another white dress.

Unlike my mother, my father enjoyed good health and was an excellent sportsman. When we were young, he encouraged us to participate in the sports that he loved, namely golf, horseback riding, and ice skating. The only sport that really interested me was golf, although I did become a good ping pong player and with the advantage of my height, excelled at basketball. As a young teenager, I started taking golf lessons with Phil Turnesa, one of the seven famous Turnesa brothers. Later, I took lessons from two of the other brothers, Mike and Jimmy. The three of them instilled in me a great love of the game, and I have been an ardent golfer to this day. In fact, once I retired from politics in the mid-1990s, I became something of a golf bum.

Despite my aversion to other sports, we were taken riding every Saturday and skating every Sunday, and I endured the misery for several years. Father also had season tickets to the New York Rangers hockey games, the New York Knicks basketball games, the New York Yankees baseball games, and the New York Giants football and baseball games in the days when the Giants played at the Polo Grounds in the Bronx and then at Yankee Stadium. He and my mother also had a subscription to the Metropolitan Opera, which I remember they attended at least once and often twice weekly.

Whenever Lou did not attend the various games, he would give his tickets to friends, relatives or business associates. Since I was a zealous Yankee fan (at one point I could tell you the batting average of every member of the team), my father would often take me to Yankee Stadium. I seem to remember always sitting in the same seats, just behind first base. For me, the most exciting baseball event was the closing weekend of the 1949 season when I was pregnant with David. The Boston Red Sox were in first place and the Yankees were one game behind. The weekend games would determine the American League pennant champion (this was before the days of play-off games). Naturally, we had to attend. Saturday was Joe DiMaggio Day, which in and of itself was an occasion for celebration, and to top the day off the Yankees won. The pennant race was then tied with one final game on Sunday. That game was another occasion we couldn't miss, but that night was also Kol Nidre, the opening service of the holiest Jewish holiday, Yom Kippur, and we couldn't be late for temple. The game was a close one and the Yankees won just in time for us to make it back to White Plains in time for services. The Yankees were champs

Growing Up

Lou, Joe DiMaggio, and Cecil Wolpa (© Bill Mark)

again, and thankfully, all the excitement had not jeopardized my pregnancy. The Yankees went on to beat the Brooklyn Dodgers, the National League contenders, for the world championship.

Those were the days of great Yankee teams and players like Lou Gehrig, Bill Dickey, Frank Crosetti, Red Ruffing, Red Rolfe, and of course, the great Joe DiMaggio, better known as the "Yankee Clipper." DiMaggio had become a great friend of my father's through a mutual friend, Max Case, a sports reporter for the *New York Journal American*. When David was about eleven years old, my father gave him a new baseball mitt. When he asked his grandfather how he should break it in, Father referred the question to DiMaggio who sent David a handwritten letter suggesting how it best be done. David was thrilled, of course. The letter was framed and has hung over his desk ever since.

My father had a large circle of friends, including the Kriendler Brothers (Mac, Bob, and Pete), the proprietors of the renowned '21' Club. It was originally a speakeasy and today it remains one of the most popular restaurants in New York City. Since my father was so close to the Kriendlers, '21' became his favorite hangout. He had

At the beach. From left - Lorraine, Norma, and Isabelle (Rose is seated behind)

lunch there three or four times a week, and after my mother died, he often dined there many evenings as well. For many years, Lou hosted a large group at '21' for New Year's Eve, in addition to his many family and business gatherings. The club was so familiar and such an important part of my family's life that '21' became known to us as "Where Else?" The ceiling of the club is covered with vans, trucks, and planes bearing the logos of favorite customers including a replica of a Health-tex truck.

Growing Up

My mother and father at a barn dance

WELLESLEY COLLEGE
3

Playing cards in our dormroom at Wellesley. I am seated center, standing behind me is Jackie Fowler and standing to the right is Lyn Rogers Jerry

Having won the Latin prize and the magnificent sum of fifteen dollars, I was graduated from high school in 1943 and left home to attend Wellesley College in September of that year. Attending Wellesley might not have happened were it not for the influence of my mother's cousin, an educator named Isadore Isenberg, known to one and all as Sokey. Late in my junior year of high school, he insisted that I come to Boston and undergo a whole battery of tests. Evidently, these tests were supposed to determine both my strengths and my limitations. Many years later, I discovered that what they predicted would be my forte was politics. Sokey convinced my father that I should apply to Wellesley, Smith, and Vassar colleges, which I did, and was accepted at all three (my children are fond of telling me that anybody could get into college in those days). I would have preferred to stay in New York and attend New York University or go to Florida and attend the University of Miami, but my father decided on Wellesley and in our family, Father's word was law, so grudgingly off to Wellesley I went. In the end, of course, he was right and that decision has stood me in good stead throughout my life.

It was while I was preparing to apply to the colleges recommended by Sokey that I first learned of Frank Sinatra. I had spent the summer at the Maxwell Summer School on the campus of Cornell University because Smith required its applicants to have either chemistry or physics coursework, and I had taken neither. I chose chemistry and was the only student in the class to pass the six-week course. The scores on the New York State Regents Exam were so low that they were all raised thirty points and I ended up with something in the high nineties.

One of the girls in my dorm at Cornell had a photo of Frank on her dresser and played his records incessantly. That was the beginning of my devotion to the singer. At my sixtieth Wellesley reunion, one of my classmates made a point to come over and say, "You were the first Frank Sinatra fan I ever knew." In fact, when the singer died, someone wrote me a condolence note. My entire family is well aware that I used to cut school and sit

Wellesley College

through three of Sinatra's shows when he was first performing at the Paramount Theater in New York (and Tommy Dorsey would hand out lemonade to those teenagers in the first few rows). When my father was able to get tickets for the radio broadcast of *Your Hit Parade*, in which Frank starred, my cousin Lorraine and I would go to almost every weekly broadcast. Sometimes we let my sister come with us, sometimes we didn't. One time, Lorraine and I hid in the ladies room so we could also attend the rebroadcast. On a few special occasions, my father and my Uncle Alex would take Lorraine and me to see Sinatra when he was appearing at a nightclub. We loved to dance with our fathers and pretend we were their young girlfriends.

I've always loved music, my favorite song being "As Time Goes By" from the film, *Casablanca*. To this day, whenever I walk into a room where one of my many musician friends is playing, that tune is immediately played. It always makes me feel right at home.

My father always had the delusion that I had musical talent. After three years of study at the Westchester Conservatory of Music, he took me to the Starlight Roof at the Waldorf-Astoria to play the piano for Leo Reichman, a friend of his who was the bandleader there. The musician, of course, disabused Father of the notion that I had the least smidgen of talent, telling him, "She's a lovely girl; she should get married and raise a family."

Two thoughts stand out in my mind about the day I was interviewing for admission to Wellesley. Sitting beside me in the waiting area was another applicant and her mother. The young woman was Jackie Loewe, now Jackie Fowler, and still a good friend. She later told me that her mother said that I would never be accepted because I was wearing a fur coat. Also, that evening I had a date with a young man from White Plains who was attending Massachusetts Institute of Technology. We had talked about going to a nightspot in Boston called the Cocoanut Grove, but for one reason or other, we changed our plans and went to another club.

Wellesley College

That was the night of the tragic Cocoanut Grove nightclub fire which took the lives of hundreds of people and injured hundreds more. When I returned to my hotel and heard about the catastrophe, I immediately called my mother who had been frantic about my safety.

In high school, I received very good grades without having to do very much work, but things were different at Wellesley. Since I had never really learned good study habits, I had a hard time my freshman year. By my sophomore year, I had developed a better understanding of how to go about my studies and then did quite well for the rest of my college career. In fact, I was invited to enter an honors program, which regretfully I never did.

Freshman year students lived in the village of Wellesley, known as the "vill," and either had to walk or ride a bicycle back and forth to campus for classes, chapel services, the library (a.k.a. the libe), and all other activities. The only exception was

Wellesley Class of '47 – Isabelle fourth row, center with Lyn Rogers Jerry to her left. Lorraine Cohen (Silberthau) is first row, seated right

our regular visits to Seiler's, the town's ice cream parlor, which was just down the street from our dormitory (Noanett), and to which we walked almost nightly for a "Wellesley Special," a brownie with vanilla ice cream and hot fudge sauce, still a favorite dessert. Some years later, the village dorms were closed down and the students now live on campus.

College life at Wellesley during the 1940s was very different from today. Dormitories were single-sex and gentlemen were not allowed above the first floor. We had to observe college parietals, which stated that we had to be in the dorm every night by 10:00 p.m., except for Friday and Saturday, when we could return by 11:00 p.m. There were also a few midnight permissions for weekends. No doubt, today's students must think of that as the Dark Ages, but such were the mores in the era during and immediately following World War II. When my grandchildren share some of the stories of what goes on in dormitories today, I am convinced that those standards were not so undesirable.

Since it was wartime, there was a shortage of help and each student had to perform a chore regularly. Sometimes we were assigned waitressing duty, which did not involve carrying heavy trays, but rather bringing in smaller platters, clearing the tables, and occasionally setting them. "Bells" duty was another assignment. At that time, intercom systems were non-existent, so we had to go to a student's room in order to notify her that she had a phone call downstairs. Moreover, students were not allowed to have cars until after spring vacation of their senior year.

In those days, I was a very good typist and my friends would often ask me to type their papers for them. Although they would offer to pay me, the recompense I preferred was that they make my bed for a certain number of days. Household chores were never my forte. I also had a friend who was very beautiful, but tended to gain weight easily. Her mother was wild when she did so and insisted that she weigh herself weekly and send the results home. The local drugstore had a scale that could be used for one cent and it would register your weight on a small card. Since we weighed approximately the same, and my weight never varied, my friend would ask me to accompany her to the village where I would weigh myself. She would then mail the card to her mom and the nagging would soon stop. My roommate, Lorraine Cohen, had another problem; she did not like to make telephone calls. Therefore, when she wanted to call a taxi or make an appointment at the hairdresser, I would have to make the call. She has gotten over that phobia and is today an inveterate user of telephones.

Earlier, I had learned the rudiments of bridge and when I got to college, I started playing a good deal. We really weren't very good, but whenever we had free time, a group of us would gather and play. Lorraine says it was then that I developed my penchant for a multitude of friendships because we always had a large, diverse group in our room.

During my years at Wellesley, Mildred H. McAfee Horton was president of the college. McAfee was the first commissioned female officer in U.S. Navy history and she was also the first director of the Navy's women's reserve called WAVES (Women Accepted for Volunteer Emergency Service). Another notable woman leader associated with Wellesley and who once visited our campus was Madame Chiang Kai Shek, the wife of Generalissimo Chiang Kai Shek, Nationalist leader of China. She attended and graduated from Wellesley in 1917 and her visit was a cause for great excitement.

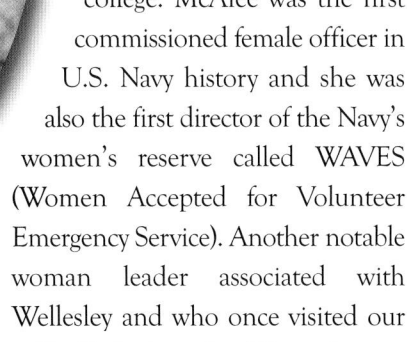

Madame Chiang Kai Shek and Mildred H. McAfee Horton, president of Wellesley College

Although I had a fine education at Wellesley, I am sure that I did not take full advantage of the opportunities offered. I am reminded of a story that once appeared in the *New York Times*. It included a comment that the moment a student entered Harvard, he was assured that certain doors would be opened to him his entire life. In a sense, the fact that I actually had graduated from Wellesley always seemed to impress people immediately, and no doubt some doors were opened for me as well.

With Father at my graduation from Wellesley College in 1947

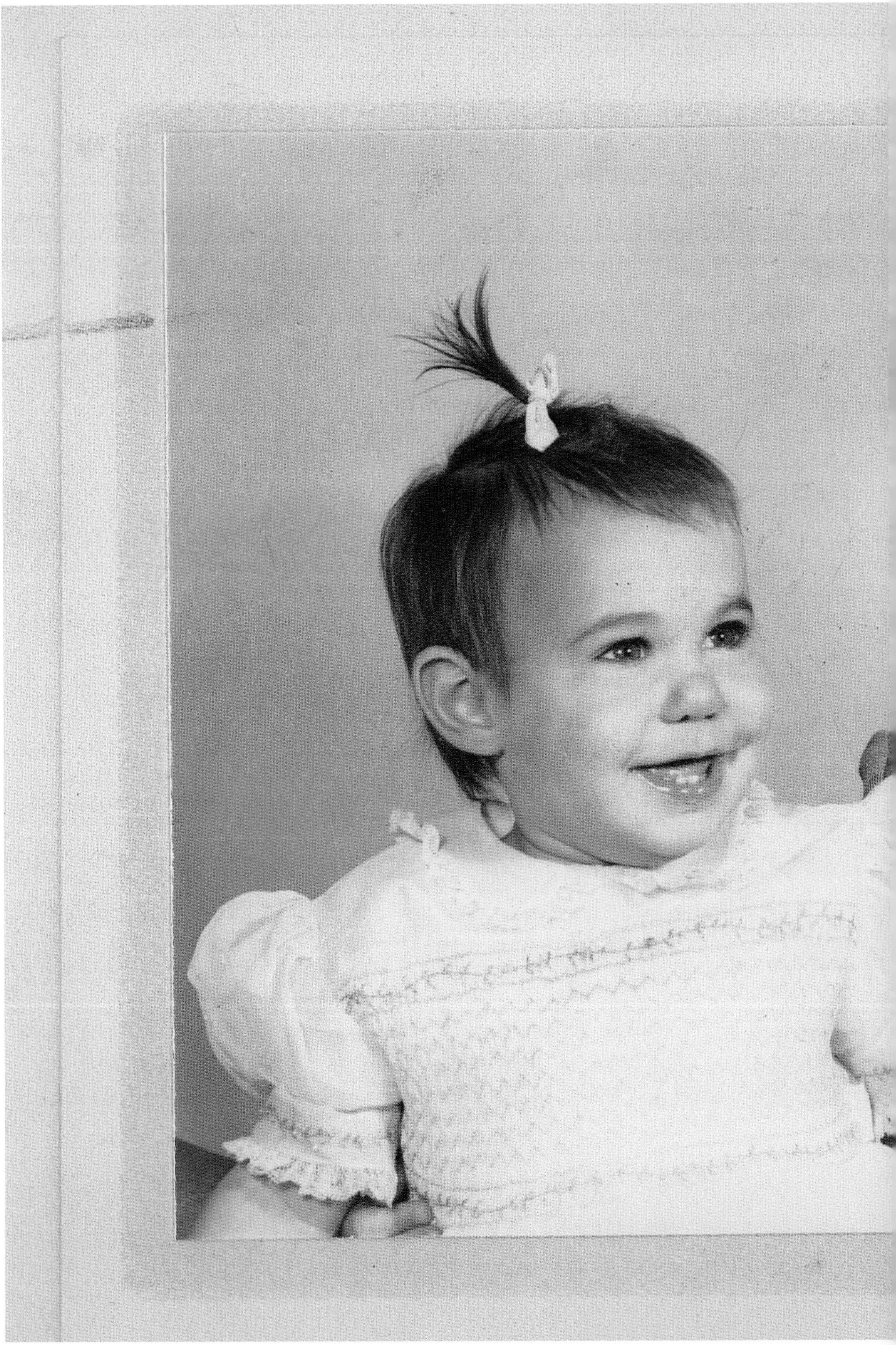

FAMILY LIFE IN RHODE ISLAND

4

*I*n February of 1947, my senior year at Wellesley, I had a blind date with Marshall Leeds. It was arranged by mutual friends of my parents and his mother. I had been seeing someone else in a rather casual way, but as soon as I met Marshall I had a feeling it would be serious. He was smart, handsome, and had a great sense of humor. He had gone to New

Family Life in Rhode Island

Isabelle & Marshall

York University and was working for Lerner Shops, a chain of clothing stores. On our first date, we went to the anteroom of the Cotillion Room at the Pierre Hotel, now known as the Rotunda. With us were my college friends, Lorraine Cohen and her fiancée, Heinz Silberthau, and Jackie Loewe Fowler who by then had married Lloyd Fowler. Marshall and I then saw each other five or six more times, whenever I was in New York for the weekend. In April, he called and said "I spoke to your father last night." "About what?" I inquired. "I asked if it was all right if I married you. Is that okay with you?" I agreed and so we became engaged. The next night the two families had a celebratory dinner at the New York restaurant Versailles with everyone present except the bride to be who was finishing up at Wellesley.

On October 19, 1947 we had a beautiful wedding at the Starlight Roof of the Waldorf-Astoria (the same site as my debut and farewell as a pianist). My sister Norma was my maid

Engagement party at Versailles (note that I'm missing). From left: David and Dotsie Spiro, Goody & Pauline Edelstein, my mother Rose, Henrietta Leeds, my father Lou, Marshall, my sister Norma, and Perry Edelstein

Family Life in Rhode Island

of honor and Marshall's sister, Doris Franklin, was matron of honor. My bridesmaids were my cousin Lorraine, college pals Lorraine Silberthau, Jackie Loewe Fowler, Lyn Rogers Jerry, and my next-door neighbor from White Plains, Marian Pierce. The best man was Marshall's cousin, Perry Edelstein. The next morning we boarded a train to Miami Beach and spent our honeymoon at the Versailles Hotel. We had talked about going to many different places, but somehow we ended up in old familiar Florida.

My sister, Norma, with her daughters, Bonnie (left) and Judy

Four years after Marshall and I wed and after she graduated from Syracuse University in 1951, Norma married Al Fields. They lived in Westchester where their daughter Judy was born in 1953, with daughter Bonnie following in 1955. Norma and Al were divorced in the late fifties and she married Murray Grabler. When Murray's former wife died a few years later, my sister inherited three young children. I always admired the way she blended the families, and to this day all the children are good friends. My niece Bonnie has always marched to her own drummer and as a teenager she became a Bahá'í, a follower of the Bahá'í Faith, whose roots date back to the mid-nineteenth century. She is excellent with languages and at one point taught English as a second language. A serious painter, she recently bought an apartment in Beijing, China, where she has a gallery and resides several months a year. Bonnie has continued her involvement with the Bahá'í community and introduced her sister Judy to one of her co-religionists, Riaz Jurney. They were married in 1991 and their son Ben was born in 1994. That youngster has always held a special place in my heart because it was on Thanksgiving Day in my apartment that his mother's water burst while resting on the couch, and Ben was born soon afterwards. A devoted mom, Judy is a lawyer and engages in arbitration work.

Marshall came from a large New Jersey family. His mother was one of four sisters and one brother and they were all extremely close. Their parents had a large summer home in Tannersville, New York, close to Hunter Mountain. Each summer all the sisters and several of their children would gather for some time together. Marshall and I spent a weekend there every summer for several years and we always enjoyed the family gatherings. After we married, he went to work for Standard Romper and we moved to Providence, Rhode Island. Our first year, we had a small furnished apartment on Everett Avenue, but soon moved to another apartment on Waterman Street. Initially, we had few friends, only Lorraine and Heinz Silberthau, Ruth and Everett Kauffman, and a couple from New York, Elaine and Marvin Neiman. During those years, I hated Providence with a vengeance and almost every weekend we would go to New York City. I constantly commiserated with the Neimans about being away from our hometown. At one point, I talked myself into a job writing a society column, "East Side News and Views," for a throwaway weekly newspaper. Since I knew virtually no one, half the items were fairy tales.

With Amy, 1957

My first dinner guests in Rhode Island were Lorraine and Heinz. I decided on a menu of cream of mushroom soup (from the can), hamburgers (the one thing I cooked fairly well), baked potatoes, peas (canned), and chocolate ice box cake for dessert. The dessert was made by purchasing a tin of chocolate cookies, arranging them in a loaf, spreading whipped cream between the layers, throwing sprinkles on top, and then cutting the loaf crosswise to make something that resembled a layer cake. I worked all day preparing the simple meal and then after dinner, left Marshall and the Silberthaus in the living room while I cleaned up—so much for making my own dinner party. I think that was the last time I ever cooked for anyone outside of my family.

I became pregnant in 1949 and we bought a house on Chase Avenue to which we moved just after our son David was born in 1950. Two years later, our daughter Amy arrived. David was so happy to welcome his baby sister that he threw a five-pound weight from the scale into her crib. Fortunately, his aim was bad. Four years later we moved to a larger home on Freeman Parkway. During our years there, we had a wonderful housekeeper named Delilah. I often accused Amy of being fonder of her than she was of me. My daughter is very sentimental and every time she is in Providence, she drives by our old house, and at one point nearly convinced her husband to buy it.

When the children were young, they fought endlessly. One of my favorite family memories illustrates their early relationship. After returning from dinner one evening with Edith and Sidney Kane, we heard screaming as we neared our front door. It was six-year-old Amy sitting on the bottom step sobbing, "I don't care what David says. I am not a 'no good fuckin son of a bitch.'" Sidney Kane fell madly in love with her at that moment and bombarded her with presents from that day forward. One of the happiest days of my life was when, not until many years later, Amy and David became good friends. I think they actually had a pretty normal and happy childhood with school, bike riding, dance lessons, and Sunday nights at

Growing up in Rhode Island, Amy & David

Ming Gardens, the local Chinese restaurant. Both children were excellent all-around athletes. They were particularly proficient at water sports and Marshall took them to swimming practice several times a week. We both attended many of the swim meets in which they participated, often successfully. To this day, one shelf in my library is filled with all of the trophies they won.

David was always very conscientious. We never had to remind him to do his homework. Amy was conscientious as well and seemed to be born independent. She was constantly off on her bicycle visiting her friends or content to be alone in the backyard shooting baskets. Until David was about seven years old, he was very difficult, while at this stage, Amy was quite docile and not too much trouble. One evening at dinner, David went screaming from the table and Marshall commented, "That certainly reminds me of when I was his age." I breathed a huge sigh of relief; I suddenly realized that David's behavior was not all my fault. Evidently, when I began to relax, his behavior began to improve. That was the moment, however, when Amy became difficult and remained so until my mother died in 1967. Apparently, the death of her grandmother affected Amy deeply and she became calmer and the arguments were fewer. When her son Matthew was going through a difficult patch she commented, "Now I know why you used to ask, 'What did I do to deserve that?'" Amy has become a very sweet, kind, compassionate, and loving person. We are best friends and her son Matthew has had the same transformation.

My favorite story about David goes back to when he was in the third or fourth grade at the Gordon School. It was a parents' night, and as I entered the classroom I saw quite a few people gathered at the blackboard, which featured the students' papers on the theme, "My Favorite Smell." David's essay was the object of much hilarity. He wrote that his favorite smell was when his mother baked bread. Everyone who knows me is aware that I rarely cook and certainly never baked. Another time, he wrote that the best dish his mother made was a corned beef sandwich. Was he trying to tell me something?

The first year that the children went to overnight camp (David went to Camp Takajo in Maine, which he attended for six years and then served as a counselor and a swimming coach; Amy went to Camp Fernwood in Maine, where she would still be a camper if it were possible), Marshall and I seized the opportunity to travel to Europe with our good friends Jewel and Larry Paley. We sailed on the *Queen Mary*, where the dining room steward informed us, "One must never order Dover Sole unless one is within sight of England." More than thirty-five years passed before I ignored his edict. On that trip we visited Paris and stayed at the Ritz, still my favorite hotel in the world, and at that time the room was only $26.00 per night. We also visited Venice, Florence, Rome, and London. It was a fabulous vacation with every sight a new adventure and with innumerable highlights. Since childhood, we had seen pictures of the Eiffel Tower, the Coliseum, the Sistine Chapel, the canals of Venice, and the magnificent art of Florence. What can be compared to the first sight of all those familiar landmarks?

Another experience concerned Her Majesty, Queen Elizabeth II. I must confess that I have always identified with her. After all, we were the same age, we each had sisters three years younger, we were married the same year, and had our first and second children the same year. Naturally, I was enamored of her, as was Jewel Paley. On several of the days that we were in London, Jewel and I would leave our husbands, get into a taxi and say, "Buckingham Palace, please." That in itself was a thrill. We would then watch the changing of the guard and wait for the queen to come out. We did this several times, but to no avail.

After a while, Marshall and I developed an active social life in Providence. Among our closest friends were Ruth and Leo Marks with whom we often went out to dinner and played bridge and golf; Jewel and Larry Paley with whom we shared the same activities; and Ethel and Al Shore. The Shores were considerably older than we were and Ethel played the role of my surrogate mother. When her daughter Marjorie remarried and later moved to New York, I assumed that role with her, although never as well as Ethel had done with me. We had a large circle of friends, among them Sylvia and Merrill Hassenfeld. Sylvia and I were friends at that time, but not nearly as close as we became when we both moved to New York and Palm Beach. In Providence, I used to say we didn't go to different parties; we went to the same party at someone else's home. Twice the Paleys joined us in giving large soirees; first, a baby party, and then a pajama party at the Health-tex plant where there was a large cafeteria.

Besides those two Health-tex party events, I generally had little contact with the company, although we always attended the company's annual outing and had a good time. The one time I did take advantage of the company's resources concerned my nomination as treasurer of the Rhode Island Wellesley Club. No one had asked me if I would undertake the position, but suddenly I was announced as the treasurer. I called the nominating committee chairman and asked, "Isn't it customary to ask someone to undertake a major position?" She replied that she had called, asked for Isabelle and had made her pitch. Suddenly I remembered that at the time I had a cleaning woman named Isabelle who told me that someone had called and talked about something financial, but that they would call again. The chairman of the committee was very persuasive, so I accepted the position. Soon, a large financial report was delivered, which I promptly stored in a cabinet, looking at it only to toss in the additional reports that kept arriving. I never really examined them. Just before the annual meeting many months later, I decided it might be a good idea to look into it. Lo and behold, I discovered that it was a very complicated double-entry bookkeeping system which had to be updated in time for the meeting. Since my mathematical ability is on a par with my musical ability, I sent it to the Health-tex office to have them decipher it. After three days it came back, nicely balanced. Of course, I declined to serve a second term.

Family Life in Rhode Island

In 1963, David celebrated his bar mitzvah at Temple Beth El in Providence. Our pediatrician, Dr Herman Marks, presented him with a Bible as a present from the congregation and said, "I hope that in the future your name will be a declarative sentence—David leads." There was a luncheon at the Biltmore Hotel and then a large party at our home that evening. The party for David's friends was held downstairs, in a wonderful basement that an artist had painted with scenes from Paris, while my family and our friends celebrated on the main floor.

David was always a good student and a good athlete. He attended Providence Country Day School and was captain of three varsity teams and editor of the school newspaper. He was also an excellent swimmer. As a senior at Country Day, he instituted a program of public service for those in the spring semester of their senior year. Each participant received credit for working on civic or communal projects. At his commencement, he was awarded the Pell Medal for History, which was presented to a outstanding graduating senior at each high school throughout the state. This was one of the few times Senator Pell came personally to present the award.

After high school graduation, David attended Harvard University where he majored in art history, a field in which he intended to pursue a career. In the spring of his senior year, however, he took a course in filmmaking and from that moment on, he was hooked on that art form. In the fall of 1972, he went off to California to take a master's degree in filmmaking at the University of California, Los Angeles. He did make one full length film called *Shoot the Sun Down* with two actors who became quite well known, Christopher Walken and Margot Kidder. The film became something of a cult flick, but was never a great financial success. David went on to work in real estate and investments and then found his true passion and became a sculptor. In 1978, he married Bonnie Badham and my first grandchild, Nicholas, was born in October of that year. I discovered that the birth of a grandchild was just about the most emotional experience a person can have, and I was fortunate enough to reach that high twice again with the birth of Amy's daughter, Stephanie, in 1986, and her son, Matthew, in 1989. When my friend and writer, Lois Wyse, was about to have her first grandchild I told her what a moving and emotional experience it was. She turned that sentiment into a column for *McCall's* magazine and later into a best-selling book called *Funny, You Don't Look like a Grandmother*. She always gave me credit for alerting her to the depth of the grandparenting experience.

David is probably one of the best fathers I have ever known. He spent a lot of time with Nicky when he was growing up, never ran out of patience with him and, in fact, was a major caregiver in his life. Bonnie had a daughter, Kelley, whom David also raised and who has become a fine young woman. Nick has inherited all of David's sweetness and I am sure he will always be very successful. He is already successful as a person; he is intelligent, warm, and friendly. He is currently working in the production end of movies and is also trying to write a film script. Nick has taken advanced education courses and in my opinion, he has the personality, temperament, and in fact, all of the qualities that would make him an outstanding member of the teaching profession. However he loves what he is doing, so more power to him.

In 1991, David and Bonnie were divorced and in 1999, David met Kathy Peck at the art studio where they both worked. They married at my home in Greenwich, Connecticut, in 2003. Kathy is one of the most competent women I have ever met. She is a gourmet cook, she paints, she sculpts, she has been a decorator, knows a lot about medicine, is a good wife and mother, and a great daughter-in-law.

Although David has always been a very concerned citizen who is interested in our country, the world, and its problems, he never became involved in partisan politics. I always thought it was because he saw too much of it while he was growing up. Late in 2003, however, he met Senator John Kerry and all that changed. David became deeply involved in his campaign and suddenly developed a passion for politics. Throughout Kerry's campaign for the Democratic nomination and then for the presidency, David was an ardent worker, arranging events and achieving remarkable success as a fundraiser. At six o'clock in the evening, Election Day, he called me from their Boston headquarters and said that Kerry was leading George W. Bush by substantial margins. Little did we realize that the next few hours would show a precipitous change. Nonetheless, the campaign was a good learning experience and he and Kathy have continued their involvement in the political world. I believe he realized once again that "Mother knows best," and that he should have listened years ago when I told him how much enjoyment politics can provide.

Like her brother, Amy was an outstanding student and athlete, and an excellent swimmer. She made the Rhode Island All-Star Basketball Team and in her senior year at Lincoln School, she was president of the athletic association. At graduation, she received an honorary student award for outstanding and consistent participation.

Amy was also a neatness freak. She would have a fit if David entered her room and would put pieces of string in strategic spots so she could tell if he had been looking into her things. She always wanted to be a teacher for underprivileged children and in fact, worked for Project Head Start in Providence. After graduating from Brown University, she took a master's degree in education at New York University, but somehow she never did work as a teacher. Instead, she found a job with the Educational Cable Consortium, which was a non-profit organization producing videotapes for families. As the assistant to the director for ten years, she participated in every phase of the company's operations including research, production, writing, and fundraising.

Amy & Anders' wedding day, 1983

During her senior year in high school, Amy had a job as a waitress at one of Brown University's eating halls. As expected, that provided her with plenty of dates with the young men at Brown, but it wasn't until much later during the summer of 1976, long after her graduation from Brown, that Amy met her husband-to-be, Anders Brag. She had been walking on Madison Avenue when she bumped into a friend of mine, Ron Rubinow, the head of Alvin Chereskin's public relations company. Ron asked her to accompany him to a cocktail party, where Anders was also a guest. Amy and Anders went together for several years until finally, in 1983, they decided to wed. They married at my home in Greenwich, Connecticut. Anders is not Jewish and Amy wanted a Jewish ceremony. He was willing to have a joint service with a rabbi, but she did not want a minister. That meant we needed a judge and although I knew judges in New York and in Rhode Island, unlike clergy, judges cannot change jurisdictions. I went to the Greenwich Library to look for a magistrate who had a Jewish name and found a justice of the peace who seemed to fit the bill.

Matron of honor on Amy's wedding day

However, when I visited him to discuss the marriage ceremony, I discovered that he was not Jewish.

The next day I happened to attend a meeting with a friend of mine, Sister Colette Mahoney, president of Marymount Manhattan College. I was early and while waiting for the others to arrive I told her about my search for a Jewish judge in Connecticut. Sure enough she knew someone whom she called immediately and who was pleased to perform the ceremony. He did a great job including having the groom stamp on the glass, the proper ending to every Jewish wedding ceremony. The wedding went off without a hitch and was very beautiful, if I do say so. I was delighted to serve as Amy's matron of honor, along with one of Anders' brothers as best man and Nicky as ring bearer. The ceremony took place in a tent off the terrace and the luncheon was held in a tent behind the dining room. It had rained for a week before the wedding, but stopped just in time for the ceremony. After all the guests had left, the rain began again. As I was preparing to go to bed, I heard a terrible crash—the ceremony tent had collapsed, pulling the poles of the terrace completely out of the concrete. I still shudder to think of what might have happened had that occurred earlier. I also hosted David and Kathy's wedding, and it was equally as lovely as Amy and Anders', although it was much smaller and took place inside. Nicky was best man and Kathy's daughter, Marissa, was maid of honor. When Kathy joined our family, it was as if I had gained a daughter and Amy had found a sister.

I always knew that Anders, being very smart, ambitious and hardworking, would be very successful. And I was right. He is interested and curious about everything and wants to see every place in the world. His family has benefited from his wanderlust as he has taken them traveling all over Europe, Africa, and the Middle East.

After her daughter Stephanie was born in 1986, Amy became a full-time mother. In addition to attending every sporting event in which her two children participated (they are both fabulous athletes), she went to every school function.

Stephanie graduated from Brown in 2008 and Matthew began his freshman year in 2007. Amy is a member of the Brown University Sports Foundation and the President's Student-Athlete Advisory Committee. She also serves on the board of trustees of the Lincoln School in Providence, Rhode Island. In addition to her work with several New York charities, she keeps busy arranging the many trips that her family takes, and oversees their homes in New York, France, Antigua, and Aspen.

Although I disliked Providence when I first moved there, I came to love it, and I can see that it was much easier to raise my children there than it would have been in New York City. I have seen Amy struggle with getting her children into the proper nursery schools and then the proper private schools. This was true in California with David's family, but to a lesser degree. These problems did not really exist in Rhode Island and I thoroughly enjoyed those years raising my children. In New York, the children have "play dates;" in Providence, they went outside to play and either walked or rode their bikes to their friends' houses, and only occasionally had to be driven to an activity. I also think that New York City children become sophisticated much too early; their childhood is of very short duration. Perhaps a fleeting childhood is part and parcel of growing up in big cities, but it is equally likely that it is a result of the times in which we live, which push our children into adulthood too quickly.

Family Life in Rhode Island

Amy's graduation from Brown University

David's graduation from Harvard University

RHODE ISLAND POLITICS
1950s - 1960s

5

*From left - Governor Frank Licht, Lorraine Silberthau,
Isabelle Leeds, and Lt. Governor J. Joseph Garrahy
(reproduced with permission from the Providence Journal Company)*

I have never fully understood how or why I became so interested in politics, but when I had my very first opportunity to choose an elective course at Wellesley, I chose political science and eventually made it my major. Perhaps it was my professor, Louise Overacker, who stimulated my interest. After graduation, I didn't necessarily consider a career in politics. In those days, most women married after college, with only a few going on to have careers. In fact, I had thought about going to law school, but I wasn't ambitious enough to commute to Boston on a daily basis.

Prior to becoming fully engaged in Rhode Island politics, I was involved in a political event that occurred in 1948. My father's lawyer, George Triedman, was a good friend of J. Howard McGrath, Attorney General of the United States. Harry Truman was running for his own term as president and McGrath arranged for me to write a campaign speech for him to deliver to the Democratic National Committee (DNC). I'm not sure what happened to that speech, but I always claimed that the president uttered words that I had written. The words I took credit for were "Good Evening, Ladies and Gentlemen." By chance, Truman was speaking in Providence the day before the election and I was invited to ride in the presidential motorcade as it drove from the airport into town. Unfortunately, there wasn't one person I knew that I could wave to en route. I stayed up virtually the entire night of the election, listening to the results, since the unexpected was happening—Truman was winning. And win he did. I had picked my first underdog candidate.

In the fall of 1952, I joined Volunteers for Stevenson. Adlai E. Stevenson, the popular governor of Illinois, was running in the presidential election against Republican opponent General Dwight D. Eisenhower. My only vivid recollection about that experience was the day that two or three of us were selected to show our support by bringing a Rhode Island Red rooster to Stevenson at his Boston headquarters—clearly, my political career started at the very top. Actually, it had started at an even lower level when as a sophomore at Wellesley I rang doorbells in Cambridge, Massachusetts, for Franklin D.

Presenting a Rhode Island Red to presidential candidate Adlai E. Stevenson (I am looking on from back)

Roosevelt's re-election for an unprecedented fourth term. I had become an admirer of the president many years earlier when I had seen him riding in a motorcade down Broadway in New York City. I had it all figured out that the blocks I had canvassed were decisive in carrying Cambridge — which was decisive in carrying Massachusetts — which of course, made the difference in the whole election. The fact that Democrats always carried Massachusetts and that Roosevelt won a resounding national victory didn't interrupt my fantasy of power.

Adlai Stevenson ran again in 1956 and I returned to work at Volunteers for Stevenson. The chairman of the Rhode Island chapter at that time was Claiborne Pell. I saw him only rarely during those years, but met him again in 1960 when he was a dinner guest at Ledgemont, a country club to which I belonged in Seekonk, Massachusetts. Coincidentally, I recall that the introduction was made by Herb Triedman, son of George Triedman, the man who had gotten me the assignment from the DNC twelve years earlier. At that time, Pell was seeking the Democratic Party's nomination for U.S. senator. He asked if I would like to do some research for him and since I loved libraries, I gladly agreed. The Democratic Party was extremely strong and Rhode Island's governor, Dennis Roberts, was the party's choice. No candidate had ever before won without the Democratic endorsement. Claiborne asked me if I thought he could win; I said no, but I would be happy to work for him anyway. Two or three weeks before the election, I went to him and said that I had changed my mind. I told him that I felt a momentum building and I believed he would be nominated. I have always thought that it was my

Rhode Island Politics: 1950s - 1960s

honest appraisal that convinced him that he could trust me to always tell him what I truly believed. Once he was the nominee, his election seemed certain and the ensuing weeks were my indoctrination into the excitement and self-fulfillment that comes with an election campaign and political life.

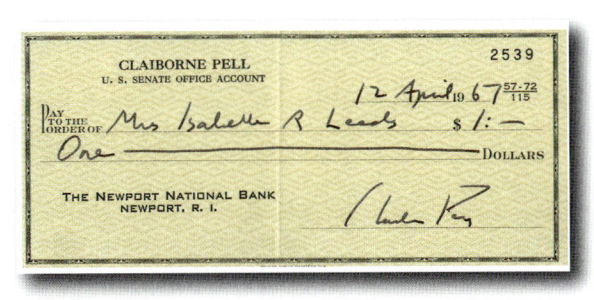

$1.00 annual paycheck from Senator Pell

After Claiborne Pell became the junior senator from Rhode Island, we all worried about getting a job. In his usual fair and honorable way, almost every campaign staff member was rewarded with a position. I was offered a spot as Research Assistant in his Providence office. When I first went to work for him, many people in Providence commented, "Oh, the Leeds must have lost their money; she had to go to work."

Actually, I was paid a dollar a year, which the Senator proudly presented to me each year. I did not seek a salaried position with Pell because I wanted the flexibility to take care of outside appointments for my family, and I wanted the freedom to travel. Throughout my political career, my financial contributions to those for whom I worked were minimal. I never wanted to feel that I was buying my job. I worked for the Senator for twelve marvelous years from 1960 to 1972.

Special Assistant to the Senator

My duties in the Providence office included research, speech writing, drafting letters to constituents, and talking with them when necessary. The job of a U.S. senator is twofold: attend to the affairs of the state and its voters, and at the same time, address the affairs of the nation. A senator's Washington staff is largely responsible for national questions of substance and the local staff generally concentrates on state affairs. In Senator Pell's office, I was fortunate to work in both areas.

I vividly remember the first speech I wrote for Senator Pell. He was to give an address at Brown University on the difference between Democrats and Republicans. His favorite analogy involved pyramids. He would say, "The Democrats believe that prosperity started at the bottom of the pyramid and drifted upward, while the Republicans believed it started at the top of the pyramid and worked its way downward." I wrote several pages on the topic and nervously awaited the evening when the speech would be delivered, but he never used it. That was my realization that Claiborne Pell rarely followed his scripts. Needless to say, I was disappointed. I always teased him that he should take public speaking lessons and then one day he was honored by a public speaking association and was awarded a plaque. He walked into my office with the plaque and a hammer in hand and nailed the award right above my desk. That was the end of my commenting on his speaking abilities. However, I am not yet convinced I was wrong.

The Senator did use a speech of mine several years later on the topic of why the United Nations was important. He had been present in San Francisco at the birth of that organization in 1945, and it was very dear to his heart. After the speech, Senator Hubert Humphrey sent Senator Pell a letter congratulating him and wrote,

> *You made a splendid defense of the United Nations, and your phrase "less Red, less dead with the U.N. than without it" is a masterpiece of political education and simplicity. I am proud of you.*

It was a moment of great pride to have Senator Pell address the Congress with the words I had written for that occasion. He very kindly sent me that letter and wrote across the page, "Isabelle, well done a wonderful phrase." I should add that all speeches given on the floor of the Senate (and even some that are never read on the floor) are entered into the

HUBERT H. HUMPHREY

United States Senate
OFFICE OF THE MAJORITY WHIP
Room G-23
THE CAPITOL

April 12, 1962

Rec'd APR 14 1962
Ans'd _____

The Honorable Claiborne Pell
United States Senate
Washington 25, D.C.

Dear Claiborne:

I noticed the attached story in the Washington Post.

You made a splendid defense of the United Nations, and your phrase "less Red, less dead with the U.N. than without it" is a masterpiece of political education and simplicity. I am proud of you.

Sincerely,

Hubert H. Humphrey

Well done — a wonderful phrase

Congressional Record, always by unanimous consent. And that speech was deposited in its entirety.

Working for the senator enabled me to pursue my many varied interests. The research I conducted for him made me an instant expert in many areas including the arts, education, public welfare, and foreign affairs. One of my favorite subjects was Tanganyika, a country in Africa that was seeking U.S. recognition of its independence. Franklin D. Roosevelt, Jr. and Claiborne Pell were appointed to represent our country and I was asked to write the speech. Unfortunately, I no longer remember anything about Tanganyika except that it was at the site of Mount Kilimanjaro. Today, it is known as the United Republic of Tanzania.

In 1964, Senator Pell appointed me to the state's advisory committee to the United States Commission on Civil Rights. As a result of urban renewal programs, entire areas of cities were razed and the inhabitants were forced to find housing elsewhere. Because housing choices were usually inadequate, this was a topic of concern for our advisory committee. The senator asked if there was anything he might do to help correct the situation. Drawing from my work with the advisory group, I was able to offer him an answer. I suggested that he propose an amendment that would put aside ten percent of the total funds allocated under the Housing and Urban Development Act to use toward affordable housing for those evicted from their homes because of urban renewal activities. New policies were created along those lines and the amendment that I suggested was incorporated. It was a matter of enormous satisfaction for me to realize that I had played even a minor part in helping to better the lives of what was probably hundreds of thousands of people.

Another interest of Senator Pell's was federal support of the arts. In our Washington D.C. office, Livingston Biddle was the key person on that subject and I provided some research assistance while he drafted the 1965 legislation that created the National Endowment for the Arts and the National

| Rhode Island Politics: 1950s - 1960s 57

Endowment for the Humanities, of which Pell was the principal sponsor. On the House side, Representative John Brademas, later president of New York University, was co-sponsor. Senator Pell was also instrumental in bringing a theater company to Rhode Island and we both became founding members of the Trinity Square Repertory Theater.

Because of his great interest in the arts, Senator Pell thought it would be a good idea for all the people of Rhode Island to be exposed to some masterpieces that they might not ordinarily be privileged to view. He assigned me the task of working with the National Gallery in Washington D.C. to develop a traveling exhibit which would be shown throughout the state. We opened the exhibition in Providence City Hall where it stayed for two weeks and then moved to other sites biweekly until it had been shown in all thirty-nine cities and towns. The project attracted a lot of attention and was very popular. On one of my trips to Washington, I accompanied the Pells to a dinner at the British Embassy and was seated next to the director of the National Gallery, John Walker. At dinner, he whispered to me, "I understand you had great success with our traveling exhibit; I can't wait until the table turns and I can talk to you about it." At that same dinner, I was saved an embarrassing moment by my other dinner partner, the artist William Walton. In those days, I was still a heavy smoker and after the first course, I opened my purse to take out a cigarette. Walton cautioned me, "At the British

Embassy, one must not smoke until after the toast to the Queen." His thoughtfulness saved me a major gaffe.

Protocol and knowledge of ceremonial precedence is something one must learn in politics. At my very first Washington dinner with the Pells, I was seated in the exact middle of the table, and guests ranking higher were seated closest to the host and hostess. During the first course, only the person at my left spoke to me. I thought it was because I wasn't important enough, but all of a sudden my right-hand partner turned and started conversing. I then realized that at political dinners, the host speaks first to the honored guest on his right and the entire table speaks in that direction. When he changes direction and speaks to his left, all the guests follow suit and turn to their other partners. In those days, women were excused after dinner and the men remained to talk and smoke their cigars. In the 1970s and 1980s, this practice was often followed at dinners I attended in New York as well, but I haven't seen it recently. In fact, if I did, I would probably refuse to leave. Because the Pells entertained a vast array of people, I was fortunate to attend many such dinners which usually consisted of a host of senators, congressmen, political commentators, and other various D.C. notables. On one trip to D.C., I also had the great privilege of attending one of John F. Kennedy's State of the Union addresses.

Claiborne Pell was instrumental in sponsoring some of our country's most significant legislation. He was one of the premier movers in developing our oceanographic resources, and it was he who first conceived of improving transportation within the megalopolis that extends from Boston to Washington D.C. He also began the efforts to modernize the railroad system in the Northeast. How well I also remember riding with him one evening on the Merchants Limited Express to New York, soon after his election, when he told me that because of his longstanding interest in foreign affairs, his ambition was to serve on the Committee for Foreign Relations and one day serve as its chairman just as his predecessor, Senator Theodore Francis

The Inaugural Committee
requests the honor of your presence
to attend and participate in the Inauguration of
John Fitzgerald Kennedy
as President of the United States of America
and
Lyndon Baines Johnson
as Vice President of the United States of America
on Friday the twentieth of January
one thousand nine hundred and sixty-one
in the City of Washington

Edward H. Foley
Chairman

Green, had done. Not only did he succeed in attaining that goal, but he also served with distinction in that post. The Senator, however, is probably best remembered as the father of the Pell Grants. The Basic Educational Opportunity Grants program passed Congress in 1972 and because of Senator Pell's advocacy, it was renamed in his honor in 1980. The program was designed to provide financial assistance to young people from low-income families so they would have an opportunity to attend college. By now, millions of students have been the recipients of these grants. It was really an honor for me to be associated with him for so many years.

One of many political gatherings. From left - Senator Pell, Nuala Pell, Arthur Goldberg, U.S. Ambassador to the UN, and Isabelle, November 1966

Claiborne had a long and illustrious career. He came from an aristocratic family after whom the town of Pelham, New York, was named. Many of his ancestors had participated in public service including one who served as vice president of the United States under James Polk. His father was a distinguished diplomat and had served as U.S. Minister to Portugal and Hungary and also served as a member of the U.S. Congress. Claiborne himself had several diplomatic stints while serving as a foreign service officer. Senator Pell is a true gentleman in every sense of the word. His wife, Nuala, is a beautiful woman and a daughter of the family that founded the A&P supermarkets. Together they are a striking couple, warm, compassionate, intelligent, and committed to serving the public good. The Pells had four children, two girls and two boys. Sadly, they lost both their son Bertie and their daughter Julia to cancer. The Senator later developed Parkinson's disease, and today is seriously handicapped, but he has never lost interest in the world around him. His legacy continues at the Pell Center for International Relations and Public Policy at the Salve Regina University in Rhode Island.

At the same time I started to work for Senator Pell, my college roommate, Lorraine Silberthau, began working for Governor John Notte. Together, we became the Peck's Bad Girls of the Rhode Island Democrats (the name was based on a fictional, mischievous character of the early twentieth century who loved to create mayhem). We knew all the politicians, pushed ourselves into meetings until our presence became accepted, and often influenced things way beyond our special responsibilities. A favorite trick of ours involved the arrival of presidential candidates. Whenever the candidates came to Providence to speak at the city hall, we didn't wait to be invited; we just marched in and stood on the platform with the rest of the pols. One of our proudest joint accomplishments was to suggest, and then help to implement, the selection of a young state senator, J. Joseph Garrahy, as state chairman of the Rhode Island Democratic Party. It was a very important position and for him, the stepping stone to becoming lieutenant governor and then governor. It was also during this time period that I served as vice chairman of the Democratic State Committee and later Democratic National Committeewoman from Rhode Island. What a host of memories I have of those days.

One highlight of those years was a state dinner in 1965 honoring Vice President Hubert Humphrey for which I was the Chairman of Arrangements (a term still in use at the time). In addition to organizing the entire affair, I wrote a song that was placed on each chair, to be sung when the vice president entered the room. It started with the words, "Loved you from the start, Hubert, bless your little heart, Hubert," and continued in a similar vein. I remember the political reporter, John Hackett, writing that no one would ever admit authorship of that song. That was the beginning of a whole range of dinners I ran through the years, no more songs, however.

That same year, Lorraine and I wrote the biography of John Capaldi, one of the candidates for Democratic Party State Chairman. He went on to be elected and became one of our closest friends and mentors. Over the years, I'm sure his secretary grew tired of seeing us in his office and looked forward to the day that a new chairman would be chosen. Little did she know that the new chairman, Joe Garrahy, was just as close a friend, as was his successor, Anthony Giannini, another good pal. Giannini was one of the smartest men I have ever known and possessed an enormous amount of common sense. He became chief justice of the Rhode Island Superior Court where he served with great distinction for many years. Lorraine and I still miss his sense of humor and his good advice. In addition to their intelligence, Anthony and John were two of the most decent and honorable men we have ever known. With John, Joe, and Anthony as our buddies, along with Providence Mayor Joe Doorley and Senator Pell, the two Wellesley girls were at the heart of all the political action in Rhode Island.

In those days, there were three powerful men who were the foundation of Rhode Island Democratic politics: Mayor Joseph Doorley, Senator Claiborne Pell, and Democratic Party State Chairman John Capaldi. Each had closer friends, but no one was as friendly as I was with all three of them. When Capaldi resigned from his position as state chairman, Lorraine and I

"One of the boys" with Anthony Gianinni to my right and John Capaldi

decided it might be a good idea for me to succeed him. John and Claiborne were lukewarm, but reluctantly agreed (they probably did so knowing full well that Doorley would never agree to it). The only thing we needed was the mayor's support. Because he wouldn't take our phone calls, we staged a sit-in at the city hall. After about two hours, he agreed to see us. We had a nice discussion, but he thought it was a terrible plan. We took his decision good-naturedly, since it really was a crazy concept at the time, but then we came up with a better scheme—why not put forth State Senator Joe Garrahy for state chairman? We left city hall and marched into the state house where we presented the idea to Joe. That was the moment his career took off, for which he still gives us full credit. He later went on to become the governor of Rhode Island.

In the mid-1960s, Rhode Island had a very popular Republican governor, our nemesis, John Chafee. We couldn't beat him in 1964 nor in 1966, though we had lots of fun trying. Then came 1968, a big year in Rhode Island politics. There were rumors that a brilliant state senator, Frank Licht, was thinking of running for governor. As a matter of fact, I had driven voters to the polls during his first campaign for state senator in 1948. Lorraine and I went to the floor of the senate one day to listen to him speak. We were very impressed, as were most members of the Democratic State Committee who were charged with the nomination process. Our friend, Joe Garrahy, was state chairman at that point and we were assigned the task of writing Licht's acceptance speech once he was nominated. Through the years, we have quoted a part of that speech hundreds of times—*If my years in politics have taught me anything, it is that you never say never.* This was significant because everyone said we could never beat John Chafee. After Licht was chosen the Democratic nominee for governor, Joe Garrahy was selected to run for lieutenant governor on the ticket. The name Licht was difficult to pronounce if you just read it, so our advertising expert, a Bostonian named Joe Manion, recorded a ditty: "L-I-C-H-T spells Licht, L-I-C-H-T spells Licht, Licht rhymes with peach, and Licht is a peach." It played constantly. It might have been corny, but it was very effective. Lorraine and I also created a monthly newsletter called the Rhode Island Review in our attempt to unseat the governor. As the campaign drew to a close, we felt that our momentum was gathering force and we had virtually closed the gap. Then a tragedy occurred; Chafee's daughter was thrown from a horse and died. We felt badly for him and badly for us, since we were sure this would derail our campaign. By a miracle of miracles, however, we won and Frank Licht became the first Jewish governor in Rhode Island history, and Joe Garrahy became his lieutenant governor. What rejoicing we did that night!

After the Licht-Garrahy team was ensconced in the state house, Garrahy asked Senator Pell if he would allow me to fill in temporarily while he staffed his office. I began working in both offices and over the next four years, I think I spent an equal amount of time in both the state house and the federal building. Lorraine had been appointed press secretary to Governor Licht and later served in that same position for Joe Garrahy after he was elected governor. She was probably the only woman to serve in that position under two different administrations.

That same year, while serving as vice chairwoman of the Democratic Party, Governor Licht appointed me Democratic National Committeewoman

From left - Governor Frank Licht, Lorraine Silberthau, Isabelle Leeds, and Lt. Governor J. Joseph Garrahy (reproduced with permission from the Providence Journal Company)

from Rhode Island, a position I held until I returned to New York in 1972. At that time, each state had one national committeewoman and one national committeeman. Today, each has several, depending on the population. Mayor Doorley was the national committeeman and we traveled together to Washington D.C. for various meetings. I found state government to be quite different from federal government, but politics is politics, regardless of location.

One of Lieutenant Governor Garrahy's major interests was healthcare and I remember writing a speech for him in 1970 or 1971 which said, "If things continue the way they are now going, soon a hospital room will cost $100 a day." If only it had actually ended at that price. In those days, Rhode Island hospitals lacked facilities for kidney dialysis.

From left - Margaret Price, vice chairman of the Democratic National Committee, Senator Pell, Eleanor Slater, vice chairman of the RI Democratic State Committee, and Isabelle Leeds (John Capaldi at microphone)

Patients who needed treatment had to travel three times a week to Boston, more than one hour each way. Garrahy asked me to research the subject and write a speech for him as a first step in developing a kidney dialysis capability in our state. As a result of his efforts, two Rhode Island hospitals were equipped with dialysis services and were able to provide treatment to those with severe kidney disease. Garrahy also played a large role in developing a six-year medical program at Brown University.

I had some interesting times working for Joe Garrahy. One night, he and I had scheduled a dinner meeting with our advertising agency executive just outside of Boston. I waited patiently for him to pick me up—it's a general rule that politicians run late, a matter of great difficulty for me since my family was always early. I do understand, however, that people are vying for their attention and it is difficult for them to turn away from potential voters. In Joe Garrahy's case, I think it was because he genuinely liked people. That day, as usual, he was very late. Suddenly, I heard a loud buzzing sound outside and knew immediately what was happening. Joe was coming for me via helicopter. All the neighbors ran outside because it was clearly landing close by. Sure enough, from a block away, in a park-like area, along came the Lieutenant Governor. I have never liked planes and helicopters even less, so I declined the offer—he could go alone or he could drive with me. Since I was a vital part of the meeting, we arrived for dinner more than an hour late.

Another great experience was when I accompanied Joe to a Lieutenant Governor's conference in Atlanta, Georgia. I can still remember my first look at Georgia's red clay soil as our plane landed. My assignment on that trip was to write down any remarks he might deliver and create press releases informing the people of Rhode Island what their lieutenant governor was accomplishing. Joe was lots of fun to travel with as he had a warm, outgoing personality, and everyone liked him. I am told that he is still warmly received every place he goes in Rhode Island. He and his wife, Margherite, have five wonderful children, all living within close proximity. Joe is a very special person. He embodies the values held by most of the people of Rhode Island.

Over the years, Lorraine and I collaborated on many speeches. We also had the assistance of a young friend, Jay Goodman, who was a master at concluding such addresses

Rhode Island Politics: 1950s - 1960s

and on whom we often called at the last minute to help us with the endings. Jay is a lawyer and a professor at Wheaton College, as well as the former chairman of the Convention Center in Providence. He was also a pollster with Elmer Cornwell, a highly respected professor of political science at Brown University. Jay remains a very astute political analyst.

Participating in Rhode Island politics was very rewarding and exciting, and never more so than when attending the conventions. In 1964, several members of the Pell staff were invited to the Democratic National Convention in Atlantic City, New Jersey, because our state's senior senator, John Pastore, was giving the keynote address. An opening had occurred for an alternate delegate, which State Chairman John McWeeney allowed me to fill. Of course, I was delighted. A brilliant keynote speech was given by Pastore; at least it sounded brilliant when you heard it in the hall. When we returned to Rhode Island, Senator Pell asked me to get a copy of the speech so that we could send it to a group of Rhode Islanders. After I read it, I realized that it was a totally pedestrian address, but what had made it spectacular was the senator's delivery.

Being a delegate at the 1964 convention enabled me to attend the reception given by Attorney General Robert F. Kennedy to thank those who had been involved with his deceased brother's campaign. The tragedy and shock of President John F. Kennedy's death the previous year kept Americans glued to their television sets for days. We watched all the sad scenes over and over—the motorcade, the race to the hospital, the swearing in of Lyndon Johnson on Air Force One with Mrs. Kennedy standing beside him in her pink, blood-stained suit, grief-stricken Bobby receiving his brother's casket, lines of citizens streaming through the Capitol to pay their respects, the procession of world leaders with Charles de Gaulle head and shoulders above all the other marchers, and three-year-old John Jr. saluting his father's casket. When Bobby Kennedy came to the podium at that 1964 convention, the crowd rose to its feet. Of all the hundreds of political events I have attended, I have never seen such an emotional and prolonged ovation as he received.

As devastating as the assassination of Kennedy was, I believe that the killing of Bobby Kennedy, nearly five years later, was more monumental in shaping the future of our nation. Bobby Kennedy almost certainly would have been elected president; he would have stopped the Vietnam War almost immediately, and we would have escaped Richard Nixon, being spared the trauma of the Watergate scandal, and on and on. I have always been impressed by the commitment to public service that the

With Senators Ted Kennedy and Claiborne Pell

Kennedy family possesses. I was saddened to learn of Senator Ted Kennedy's sudden illness and together with the rest of America, pray for him and the entire Kennedy family.

I remember one evening when Ted Kennedy was the guest of honor at a gathering I attended in the home of Joe and Margherite Garrahy. That night many photos were taken of him with supporters. When it came time for his departure, he thanked everyone and began walking down the path to the driveway. He then stopped, turned around

Rhode Island Politics: 1950s - 1960s

and said, "I've had my picture taken with everyone but Isabelle. Let's do that now," and we took a photo together. In 1970, one of his lieutenants called and asked if I would serve as chairman of his reelection campaign for one of the local Massachusetts' chapters. I regretfully declined; it was my belief that an out-of-state resident should not serve in that capacity.

The next convention I attended was held in Chicago, Illinois, in 1968. There had been two major Democratic candidates, Senators Robert Kennedy and Hubert Humphrey, with Eugene McCarthy as a third possibility. I had been a delegate for Senator Kennedy, but when he was assassinated in June of that year, I was forced to be committed to Humphrey. I was also appointed to represent Senator Pell on the Credentials Committee.

There was a good deal of dissention about the seating of opposing delegations from a few of the southern states. It was the job of the Credentials Committee to recommend the proper course of action for the entire convention. That necessitated my arriving a few days early to attend committee meetings. I flew out with Mayor Joe Doorley, John Capaldi who was then Racing Commissioner, and State Senator Bob Maggiacomo.

Larry O'Brien, chairman of the Democratic National Committee during the Kennedy Administration

In the mornings, we attended meetings and during the afternoons and evenings we were usually free. The men were very considerate, including me in everything they did. We had lunches, attended the races, went to cocktail parties and dinners, and generally had a ball for three days before the convention started. Many of the festivities and all of the transportation were provided by the citizens of Chicago as a part of their civic contribution.

In one of the early sessions of the convention, we had to spend the entire day in the assembly hall because of the dispute over the inclusion of a peace plank in the party platform. The Kennedy and McCarthy people wanted to include a plank calling for an end to the Vietnam War. The Humphrey people wanted no such thing, viewing it as a slap in the face to President Johnson. We had to sit through the debate all day and into the evening, with dinner served at our seats, courtesy of Kentucky Fried Chicken. Consequently, I was never able to hear any of the news reports about the fighting that was taking place outside the convention hall between the peace protestors and the Chicago police. When a Rhode Island reporter asked me what our delegation thought about Chicago, I could only speak about the great hospitality we had been shown over the past few days. What an embarrassment when I finally heard what was really going on. In addition, our delegation had voted against the peace plank and our group's chairman, Mayor Doorley, knowing that I supported it, thought it would be amusing for me to announce the results to the floor of the convention. I was not amused.

Making the peace plank announcement at the 1968 Democratic Convention

Rhode Island Politics: 1950s - 1960s

Another of my clearest memories of that convention was the sight of Connecticut Senator Abraham Ribicoff on the dais pointing his finger at Mayor Richard J. Daley of Chicago and shouting, "How the truth hurts! How the truth hurts!" He was referring to news accounts and accusations that the mayor used undue force to keep the crowds outside of the convention hall under control.

I also attended the 1972 Democratic Convention in Miami as a delegate because of my position as national committeewoman. That was the year in which there was so much wrangling and so many long speeches that George McGovern's acceptance speech was not delivered until two o'clock in the morning, thereby eliminating any possibility of a large audience. Through my friend Alvin Chereskin, I had received a commission from *Mademoiselle* magazine to do a story on women attending the convention. I interviewed many female delegates, some of them well known, some unheard of. Congresswoman Bella Abzug, who was a New York delegate, observed that women at the 1972 convention compromised nearly 40% of the convention body as compared to only 13% in 1968, and they were better represented on the individual delegations and committees as well. The piece I wrote for the magazine appeared in the November 1972 issue.

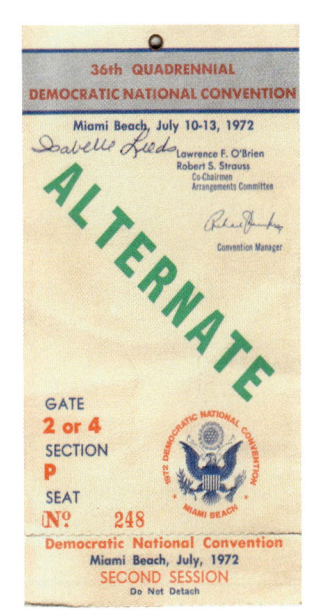

By 1976, I had moved back to New York and was an alternate delegate to the Democratic National Convention held at Madison Square Garden, which nominated Jimmy Carter. I was again a delegate in 1980 where I supported Ted Kennedy against President Jimmy Carter. Unfortunately, Carter was renominated and that November, for the first and only time in my life, I did not vote for the Democratic presidential nominee. I could not vote for Ronald Reagan nor could I vote for Carter who I thought had done a poor job as president, so I cast my protest ballot for the Independent candidate, John Anderson. In 1984, I was in Europe and did not attend the convention, but in 1988, I went to San Francisco as a member of the Democratic National Finance Committee. It was there that Mario Cuomo gave the magnificent speech that propelled him into the spotlight as a potential presidential candidate. I have never understood why he didn't run for the office. What a president he would have been.

Later, in the spring of 1992, I attended a large meeting in Washington with Democratic presidential candidate, Bill Clinton, and his early supporters. After I was introduced to him and after a bit of polite conversation, I said, "I think I know how you can get Mario Cuomo to support you." Naturally, he was interested since Mario's support as governor of New York would be very meaningful. "Tell him you will appoint him to the Supreme Court" I advised. Within twenty-four hours, I heard a similar statement repeated in the press. I have always wondered if my suggestion that night triggered the news story. As it turned out, Cuomo announced that he would not accept a nomination to the Supreme Court. He would have made a superb justice. My final two conventions were in 1992 and in 1996, where I was not a delegate, but an "honored guest" because of my work in the Clinton campaigns.

Although I was involved in politics when women were not well-represented in the field, I never considered myself a feminist politician nor did I have any dealings with the women's movement. I didn't think of myself as a woman in politics; I thought of myself as a politician who happened to be a woman. I favored women's equality, of course, but it was never a major issue with me, perhaps because I was not subjected to unequal pay or even unequal treatment. Lorraine and I were always considered "one of the boys," and we were included in all kinds of political strategy meetings and other gatherings. I never accepted a paid position because I wanted the freedom and flexibility to care for my children, get them to their appointments, and have time for my other acitivities and interests. I returned to work only after my children began school, and I was fortunate to have a housekeeper to greet them when they returned home. I believe my children benefited from my political work. Their horizons were expanded at an early age and they were kept abreast of current events. They were often exposed to interesting people who they would have never met nor known without my involvement in politics. They also learned how politics significantly affects people's everyday lives. I enjoyed my political work in Rhode Island, and I can recall commenting in my 15th Wellesley reunion class book that I was delighted that I no longer had to respond as "housewife" when faced with the question of "occupation."

"I LOVE NEW YORK"
Political Life in New York City, 1970s-1995

6

*Charlotte, Isabelle, Phyllis & Susan's NY, NY:
A Woman's Guide to Shops, Services and Restaurants*

The year 1967 was my *annus horribilus*. On March 1st, my mother died; there's no need to say what sadness that brought. Then, although we had spent many happy years together, my marriage to Marshall started to disintegrate. By 1970, we were divorced. I know my children were unhappy about that situation, but I can honestly say that I don't believe they ever heard either one of us say anything nasty about the other. Shortly thereafter, Marshall retired from Health-tex and after a few years in New York, he moved to Boca Raton, Florida. We see each other with the children occasionally and there is no animosity between us.

At the end of that year, I decided I would go back to my New York roots, at least partly, so my father bought me a small apartment at the Lombardy Hotel on 56th Street, just off Park Avenue. I planned to spend half my time there and the other half in Providence. Before I could put that plan into effect, however, I had an emergency operation to remove an ovary. The recuperation was slow, and shortly after I recovered, I discovered a lump on my breast that fortunately turned out to be benign. But it necessitated another surgery to ascertain that. As soon as I felt better, I began spending more and more time in New York and soon realized that it was there that I wanted to live full-time. In October 1971, I found a wonderful apartment on Park Avenue into which I moved a year later, and which has been my New York base for thirty-five years and counting.

One day in December 1971, I accompanied my father to the bar mitzvah of the son of Alvin Chereskin, the head of AC&R Advertising, the company that had done the famous Health-tex ads. Seated beside me was an attractive gentleman named Bill Hill with whom I conversed for a bit during the services. That evening when we returned to Long Island for the dinner that followed the event, Bill asked me to dance several times and then asked if he could call me. He called the following day and we started seeing each other whenever we were both in New York. At that time, although he had an apartment in New York, he lived in St. Louis, Missouri, and

"I Love New York"

One of many good times with Bill

Isabelle & Bill Hill

traveled a great deal because of his business. In the spring of 1972, we went to Europe together with Alvin and Susan Chereskin. We stayed at the Grosvenor House in London where we were introduced to several clubs for dining and gambling by Binnie Barnes, an old-time British movie actress who resided there. We had a wonderful time in London, and in Paris as well, where we stayed at L'Hotel on the Left Bank, a marvelous small establishment which had been the home of Oscar Wilde. I was particularly impressed with two facts about the hotel: all the furnishings were beautiful antiques and each day all the towels and robes in the bathroom were changed to a different Porthault pattern. We traveled to Europe several other times and later to Hong Kong where Bill had business interests. Bill was a brilliant man and could talk to anybody about anything. At the many receptions and dinners that I had to attend because of my job, he was always a wonderful companion, knowledgeable about every country and issue that was under discussion. Often his scientific explanations would leave me far behind, but his business advice was invaluable to me when I later undertook a fashion project for the governor of New York. Bill was a kind and gentle man and we had a close and loving relationship for many years, until he decided he wanted to move back to Texas. That was an impossible concept for me, and so we parted, but have remained good friends.

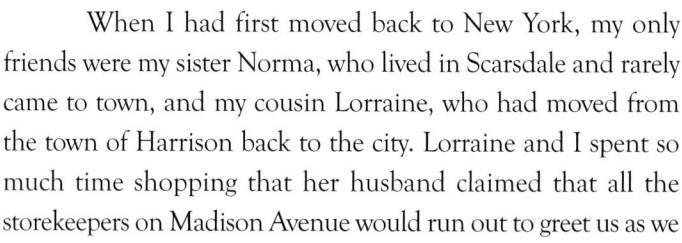

When I had first moved back to New York, my only friends were my sister Norma, who lived in Scarsdale and rarely came to town, and my cousin Lorraine, who had moved from the town of Harrison back to the city. Lorraine and I spent so much time shopping that her husband claimed that all the storekeepers on Madison Avenue would run out to greet us as we

"I Love New York"
Political Life in New York City, 1970s-1995

walked by. I soon grew tired of that, however, and one day discussed it with Alvin Chereskin. In addition to his advertising business, he also had a small public relations company and asked if I would like to work there. I jumped at the chance and began immediately. The head of that division was Ron Rubinow, the bright young man who had invited Amy to the cocktail party at which she met her husband, Anders. The most memorable account I worked on was that of a cruise company that was launching the *Stella Solaris* out of Fort Lauderdale, Florida.

My assignment was to arrange the opening party for the ship's maiden voyage. It involved a trip to Palm Beach to meet with the chairman of the charity that would be the beneficiary of the event and to coordinate the details. I met with the chair, Alexandra Landa, who in later years became the constant companion of a close pal of mine, Elliot Schnall. Once we got started on the project, we realized that what we needed was "social" public relations, which our firm did not do. So we subcontracted that part of the job to Budd Calisch, who had a small public relations company in New York. His responsibility was to get the maximum social press coverage and he excelled at the assignment. We had on board the cruise ship Eugenia Shepard, the syndicated fashion columnist for the *New York Post*, and Aileen Mehle,

Enjoying the company of Budd Calisch and Susan Fine

who wrote the widely-syndicated social column, "Suzy," for the *New York Daily News* and later wrote for the *Women's Wear Daily*. At the time, they were the two most influential social columnists in New York, if not in the country. In addition, there were several writers who covered for other press. The event was a great success, attracted quite a few socialites, and gained wide media coverage. I met many people who would later become good friends including Stephen Stempler, an interior designer who became one of my closest friends and eventually decorated my home in Palm Beach; Susan Fine (now Susan Burke), with whom I collaborated on a book; Dorothy Hammerstein (widow of the great composer Oscar Hammerstein) who used to spend time with me (or even once without me) at my home in Greenwich; Budd Calisch; and several others.

Dorothy Hammerstein & Mildred Fields

A few months after I began work at AC&R, my father's friend and physician, Dr. Kevin Cahill, called and said he would like to bring his buddy, Congressman Hugh Carey, to meet me. This was in early 1974. We arranged breakfast at my home for 8:30 a.m. one morning that following week. After about three quarters of an hour, Dr. Cahill left and Congressman Carey stayed on. He knew about my work in Rhode Island and told me he was thinking of running for governor the next year. We continued talking politics through lunch until mid-afternoon. His wife was very ill, and he said he would not make the decision for a while. Shortly thereafter, we were all together again at a dinner of the Appeal of Conscience Foundation, a group on whose board I served, and heard that Nelson Rockefeller would not seek another term as governor. I think that might have been the catalyst for Carey's decision

Kevin and Kate Cahill with my father, Lou

"I Love New York"
Political Life in New York City, 1970s-1995

to run. A week later, he invited me to lunch with his brother Edward and a lawyer, Jerry Wilson. During the course of the conversation, Carey said to Jerry and me, "I would like the two of you to be the co-chairs of my campaign for governor." I was both flabbergasted and delighted since I much preferred politics to public relations. In a sense, the two are not that different from each other; work for politicians involves ensuring that they are seen in the best possible light and the same is true of public relations.

Howard Samuels and Ogden Reid, both well-known New Yorkers, had also announced their candidacies for the Democratic nomination. I called Senator Pell for his advice. He told me that Carey didn't have much of a chance, but he could get me a job with either Samuels or Reid. I said, "I think I'd rather be a general in a losing campaign, than a foot soldier in a winning campaign." Voila! I had picked another dark horse and ended with a victorious candidate. Later, I remember a U.S. senator visiting the governor's office who put his finger on my shoulder and said, "I'd like to touch you for luck."

I must admit that I did not have too many real responsibilities in the campaign, since I was a relatively recent New Yorker, without too many political connections. After Carey won the primary, the general campaign was almost anticlimactic, because New Yorkers usually elect Democrats. I had great fun, nonetheless, putting together a citizens' committee for Carey and working on a concert at Madison Square Garden to benefit the Carey

Isabelle with Bob & Phyllis Wagner

campaign. Tony Scotto, who was head of the Longshoreman's Union, and Phyllis Cerf, who was dating former New York mayor Robert Wagner, were the main powers arranging the affair. The star attraction was Frank Sinatra. He and Phyllis were close friends and she gave a party for him at her home and invited many of those working on the event. She introduced me to him by saying, "Isabelle was one of your early bobbysoxer fans," to which he blandly replied, "Oh." After the campaign, Phyllis and Bob married and Frank was the usher who showed me down the aisle. I later saw him many times at the Wagners' home, as well as at the home of Judy and Bill Green, other close friends of the singer's. He was always very nice to me, offering to do a walk-on for my son David's next film (which David never made) and suggesting how his lawn could be improved, since they both lived in the same area of Beverly Hills.

I must have attended dozens of, if not one hundred, personal appearances by Sinatra. There were always enthusiastic audiences present, but the most thunderous ovations always occurred when he would sing *New York, New York*. On one such occasion, Frank's wife, Barbara, was chairperson of a benefit that was held in the ballroom of the Waldorf-Astoria, where he was the main attraction. Governor Carey attended the event and invited me to join his group. As Frank was preparing to conclude his performance, he walked over to a spot just below our table and announced, "I would like to dedicate this number to the Governor and his guests." He proceeded to sing *New York, New York*, and needless to say, that was the best rendition of the song I had ever heard.

In the summer of 1974, at the suggestion of my new friend Susan Fine, I took a week off from the Carey campaign to spend seven days at the Golden Door, a spa in Rancho Santa Fe, California. At that time it was very small and unpretentious and had a fabulous exercise program. I had never done a day's exercise in my entire life and at the end of that first day, I ached in muscles I was not even aware of having. I called Susan and said, "I thought you liked me. How

"I Love New York"
Political Life in New York City, 1970s-1995

could you send me here?" By the end of the week, however, I had lost five pounds, many inches, and felt marvelous. I returned for twenty more years and always considered my visit to the spa as one of my favorite weeks of the year. In addition, several of the women that I had met there are still good friends. Today, the Golden Door is much larger and very elegant. In my mind, both then and now, it is the best spa in the United States.

I knew that I could have almost any job in the Carey administration that I requested, but I didn't know what to ask for. My friend, Angier Biddle Duke, found the perfect position for me—Special Assistant to the Governor for International and United Nations Affairs and Chief of Protocol for New York. What a splendid eight years followed!

At the time, Angie was commissioner of civic affairs and public events for New York City. He had previously served as President Kennedy's chief of protocol and as ambassador to El Salvador, Spain, Denmark, and Morocco. He taught me what my job entailed and how to best undertake the duties. I soon became very friendly with Angie and his wife, Robin, who incidentally is one of the most beautiful, articulate, and capable

From left - Angier Biddle Duke, Isabelle, Stanley Love, Barbara Fife, and Leonard Lauder

women I have ever known. Toward the end of the Clinton administration, Robin served as our ambassador to Norway. Unfortunately, Angie died a few years ago at age eighty when he was rollerblading in Southampton, New York, and was struck by an automobile. His funeral at St. John the Divine Cathedral was the largest outpouring I have ever seen outside of a political funeral I once attended at St. Patrick's Cathedral in New York.

As defined in my official job description, my major responsibility as special assistant was to represent the governor to the total international community, including the United Nations, the Consular Corps, and any visiting personages from overseas, be they kings, queens, presidents or prime ministers. I was expected to help solve any problems that international residents of New York may have with the various agencies of state government. In consultation with the U.S. Department of State, I was to make recommendations on the appropriateness of issuing proclamations on behalf of different ethnic constituencies and make suggestions as to the wording when such proclamations were issued. As chief of protocol for the state, I was required to greet important visitors on their arrival here, set up any meetings the governor had with representatives of foreign governments, accompany him on those visits, and organize any receptions he may decide to hold in their honor. My duties also included drafting responses to correspondence from any and all non-Americans, and acting as state director of the Friendship Force and overseeing all New York efforts in that area.

During those years, I was fortunate to have the secretarial services of Joyce Gleit who worked in the governor's New York office. Joyce was a part-time novelist and had published several books, but politics was her first love. She was cheerful, willing, very efficient, and made my job much easier. We still remain friends. During Carey's first term, the New York office was run by Erica Teutsch and then Carol Sherman who took over during his second term. Erica and Carol were both very organized, talented women.

One of the most interesting experiences I had as chief of protocol was associated with Governor Carey's decision to meet

"I Love New York"
Political Life in New York City, 1970s-1995

with Anwar Sadat, the president of Egypt. I was assigned the task of arranging the meeting and I conferred by phone with my counterpart in the Egyptian delegation. We agreed that the meeting would take place at the Waldorf-Astoria in New York City. Part of the agreement was that there would be no photographs, since meeting with the Egyptian president might create political unrest with the large Jewish electorate in New York. The meeting was scheduled for 9:00 p.m., but as the meeting time neared, telephone calls started coming from Sadat's hotel room. They wanted photos although we had agreed that none would be taken. The negotiations went on for an hour and finally Carey declared that the meeting was canceled. Fortunately, I had acquired the habit of making copious notations of every telephone conversation I had on the governor's behalf and I was able to reassure him that the agreement had been "no photos." I don't recall any repercussions from the canceled meeting. In fact, I had Mrs. Sadat at my home a few years later after her husband had been assassinated. I recall that she was charming and intelligent.

In my position with the Carey administration, I also did a number of things not connected with the international field. These included drafting replies to personal correspondence and ensuring that any necessary thank you notes were written. I was also required to maintain a liaison with fundraising efforts in the state. Although I do not enjoy fundraising and do not feel particularly good at it, I did have some experience and success just prior to being offered the position with Carey. Brown University President Donald Horning had asked me to chair an effort to raise funds for a new theater at the school. The committee was so successful that the new theater

Stephanie, Amy, and Matthew in front of the Leeds Theater, Brown University

was named the Isabelle Russek Leeds Theater, although most of the work was done by a great staff member, Mimi Wolk, and by Richard Salomon, who I believe was chancellor of the university at the time. I was then invited to become a member of the Corporation of Brown University, which consists of a board of fellows and a board of trustees. I served on the latter for six years. Although I attended all of the board meetings, the demands of my full-time job with the governor made it difficult for me to travel to Providence for the many committee meetings, which was where the real work of the board was done. I did manage to attend a few of those sessions, which were chaired by John Nicholas Brown, one of the most respected citizens of Rhode Island and a man of enormous charm and wit, as well as intellect. His meetings were always great fun and very productive.

Part of my responsibilities as chief of protocol involved greeting heads of state when they arrived at JFK Airport. Kevin Cahill, who had introduced me to Governor Carey, had been appointed Special Assistant to the Governor for Health Affairs, an office he performed with extraordinary ability. Dr. Cahill was not only a fine physician, he was an internationally renowned humanitarian, a beautiful writer, the longtime president of the American Irish Historical Society, and one of my closest friends. His beautiful wife, Kate, who unfortunately died a few years ago, was a potter, a poet, a photographer, and a person of unusual kindness and generosity. Kevin believed that the cars the state provided me for my trips to the airport were not suitable for distinguished guests. He had inherited a huge sedan from the estate of Norman Norell (a leading American couturier) that was so large that we dubbed it the "Black Maria" and that became my transportation for a year or so before it broke down completely, and I was happy to see it go.

As chief of protocol for the state, I got to know Marifé Hernandez, who was chief of protocol at the United States Mission to the United Nations. We soon became, and still remain, the best of friends. My first meeting with Marifé was amusing. Her husband at the time, Foxy Carter, worked at the

"I Love New York"
Political Life in New York City, 1970s-1995

U.S. Mission to the UN, a Gerald Ford appointment. When I saw him at a Jimmy Carter fundraising event, I asked what he, a Republican, was doing there. He replied that his wife was a great supporter of Carter's and introduced me to Marifé. We instantly became good acquaintances, but on our 1980 trip to Paris on behalf of the upcoming New York Fashion Market World Buyers Week we became firm friends. This occurred over a late lunch of bread and cheese and wine at a small hotel on the rue du Faubourg Saint-Honoré. We are now so close that she calls me her "Mother Superior" and is very likely to take my advice in many matters. In 1999, she married Joel Bell, a Canadian and a wonderful gentleman, who had been Canadian Prime Minister Pierre Trudeau's chief economic advisor. The first time I met Joel, I told Marifé that she must marry him. Marifé has long served on the board of New York Hospital, now New York-Presbyterian Hospital, and she is my authority on medical care at that great institution. The merger of those two hospitals has been one of the very few such combinations that has worked brilliantly.

In my position, I also got to know Daniel Patrick Moynihan, the United States representative to the UN, fairly well. When he decided to run for the Senate in 1976, I was asked to give a fundraiser for him. I was always happy to offer my home and to provide refreshments for such functions, but providing the guests was not my specialty. The committee agreed to those terms and asked if I had a piano because they wanted to ask Cy Coleman, the well-known composer of many hit tunes, to entertain at the event. It so happens that I have a Beckstein concert grand piano, which incidentally, was the last bargaining chip in the purchase of my apartment because it was too large to remove. Between the dynamic personality of Pat Moynihan and the great music of Cy Coleman, the party was a huge success. Pat went on to win a heated primary and then the election, and became one of the great senators of our time.

Because of my job in the Carey administration and my simultaneous membership on the board of the Appeal of Conscience Foundation, I was asked on another occasion to chair a luncheon for the Empress of Iran, Farah Pahlavi, also known as Farah Diba. The event was held at the ballroom of the Pierre Hotel and was the occasion of a giant protest outside the building. It was very unpleasant, and even a little frightening, to hear the chants and catcalls from the street. My niece, Bonnie Fields, who is a Bahá'í, had chastised me for participating in an honor to the Iranian Empress. It is also possible that she had been part of the protest group outside the hotel. Bonnie's resentment of the Shah, the Empress's husband, stemmed from her conviction that the Bahá'ís were being persecuted in Iran for their beliefs.

At the request of Governor Carey, I also hosted a reception for the Prime Minister of Israel, Yitzhak Rabin. It was quite a coincidence that I had diplomatic dealings with both Sadat and Rabin, the two martyred leaders of the Middle East. For the reception, most of the leaders of New York's Jewish community were invited, as well as a few of my friends. At the party, my sister overheard an Israeli security guard say, "Isn't it nice of Mrs. Leeds to do this for us and she isn't even Jewish." I wonder what happened to the vaunted Israeli intelligence service in this case.

Since I represented the governor at many events that he himself could not attend, I became friendly with many of the UN ambassadors. One of the most interesting was Fereydoun Hoveyda, the ambassador from Iran. I was at the Iranian Embassy so many times (this was during the Shah's reign and our two countries were very friendly) that the waiters soon learned of my fondness for caviar. They would come over to me with huge containers and say to the surrounding guests, "You'll have to wait until Mrs. Leeds is finished." I'm well aware that all the

With Rosalie Levine

"I Love New York"
Political Life in New York City, 1970s-1995

gracious service I received was not due to my great charm, but because I represented the governor. It was fun nonetheless.

Ambassador Hoveyda was a fine artist and he gave me several of his watercolors. One of the couples I met at his home and to whom I became very close were Rosalie and Joe Levine. Joe was the famous producer of such movies as *The Graduate*, *A Bridge too Far*, *The Day of the Dolphin*, and many other blockbuster films. They lived in Greenwich, Connecticut, in a magnificent house that had a large and well-equipped screening room. Attending a movie at their home soon became one of my favorite weekend activities. Joe also had a collection of several antique cars, which intrigued my friend Bill Hill whose hobby was restoring such cars. Unfortunately, as much time as we spent with the Levines, we never did view that collection. Rosalie was a great hostess and was responsible for all of the lavish opening night parties occasioned by a new film. I considered Joe one of my nearest and dearest friends and delivered one of the eulogies at his funeral. I never could reconcile the pussycat I found him to be with the ferocious lion I knew it took to succeed in show business.

Another couple with whom I became friendly were Kurt Waldheim, former UN Secretary-General, and his wife, Cissy. Not only was I invited to their beautiful residence on Sutton Place as a representative of Governor Carey, but I was often invited to many of their private celebrations. Also, whenever we were all at Claridge's in London, we would have tea or a drink together. I gave a black tie dinner for the couple at my home in which some of the guests were Patricia Kennedy Lawford, Arthur and Alexandra Schlesinger, Ted and Gillian Sorenson, Angie and Robin Duke, and about sixteen other prominent New Yorkers. Clearly, the Waldheims were very socially and politically acceptable at that time, so you can imagine my horror when Kurt Waldheim was accused of being linked to Nazi atrocities. They had always been warm and friendly toward me and I never saw the slightest tinge of antisemitism. After they had left New York and he had been elected president of Austria, I never saw or heard from them again.

As chief of protocol, I dined at many UN embassies and consulates. The place I visited most often was the home of Israeli Ambassador Chaim Herzog and his wife, Aura. They were extraordinarily effective in winning over the press and other influential opinion makers. He later became the sixth president of the state of Israel.

In addition to representing the governor at receptions and public events, I also attended meetings on his behalf. At one such meeting, I was to inform the consuls general of Great Britain and France that Governor Carey was not happy about the prospect of the Concorde jet landing in New York. His opposition stemmed from the fact that the noise over Nassau County and near the airport would be very upsetting to those New Yorkers living in those areas. Upon hearing Carey's concern, the British consul general commented, "I'm glad we've passed the days when the messenger who delivered bad news was punished." Little did he know that I favored the arrival of the supersonic plane. Some time later, of course, an agreement was reached and the era of the Concorde began.

When one lives a hectic life in New York City, weekend and summer respites become highly desirable. In 1976, I decided to go house hunting in Greenwich, Connecticut, where my sister had a home. I was lucky enough to find a place on Glenville Road which continues to be my weekend haven and where I still spend the entire summer. After working for months with Charles Dear, the decorator who did my New York apartment, I spent my first weekend there in April of 1977. My first house guests were Jeanne and Bill Amory, and Mildred Hilson.

During the first few years at my Greenwich home, I went back to playing tennis since there was a court on the property, but finally decided that I would never be a good tennis player. Golf was my sport and that's what I returned to. Fortunately, about that time, I was invited to join Century Country Club in New York where I made many good friends. I am still a dedicated golfer and refuse to acknowledge that at my age I

"I Love New York"
Political Life in New York City, 1970s-1995

will never regain the game that I had in my thirties and forties, but I continue to strive for that goal.

Swearing in as Special Assistant, from left - Hugh Carey, Amy, Isabelle, Lou, and Norma (© Impact Photo, Inc.)

The 1976 Bicentennial celebrating the independence of our country was a year of great activity for everyone involved in government. A few major events took place that summer. The first was the visit of Her Majesty Queen Elizabeth ll and Prince Philip to New York. Governor Carey and I met the Queen and Philip upon their arrival aboard The Royal Yacht *Britannia*. As we made our way down to the pier, the British consul general announced that "Governor Carey will escort Her Majesty and Mrs. Leeds will escort Prince Philip." One of the earliest lessons Angie Duke had taught me was never to curtsy when greeting royalty; this is a no-no for Americans. Nor does one shake hands with the queen unless she offers her hand first, which she did on this occasion and I imagine most others. We addressed the queen as "Your Majesty" and Prince Philip as "Your Highness." It was a rather long walk back to the car and Philip walked the entire way with his hands clasped behind his back. He would walk over to the crowds behind the ropes and speak to them, but never shake hands. He and I had very little conversation. I found him as cold and forbidding as the queen was warm and at ease.

One of the places that Her Majesty had always wanted to visit was Bloomingdale's, and a trip there was arranged. But a problem arose. The store occupies an entire square block between East 59th and 60th Streets, and Lexington and Third Avenues. It is a rule that the queen always exits a car from the right-hand side; Lexington Avenue, however, runs south, while Third Avenue, at the other entrance to the store, runs north. In neither case could she exit properly. The problem was solved by closing a few blocks of Lexington Avenue to traffic and making it run uptown for several blocks. The proper protocol was observed and Her Majesty was able to exit the car from the right side.

Another stop with the queen was a luncheon at the Waldorf-Astoria, which was uneventful compared to the evening festivities that were planned. As chief of protocol, I was invited to the party that the royals were giving aboard the *Britannia*. I was accompanied that evening by Mr. and Mrs. John Loeb. Mrs. Loeb, known as "Peter," was chairman of the New York City Commission for the United Nations and Consular Corps and we very often worked together as colleagues. We also played golf and bridge together, lunched, had dinner, and took in an occasional movie. Also with us that night was the Mayor of Jerusalem, Teddy Kollek. You can imagine my delight at spending the day and evening with the queen, my childhood idol. I found her prettier than her pictures and charming to talk to. I also remember her chatting with each and every guest. My head was so far in the clouds that I can't remember any part of our conversation.

"I Love New York"
Political Life in New York City, 1970s-1995

Many foreign leaders and royalty visited New York that summer including the Emperor of Japan, the King of Norway, and the Queen of Denmark. After the King of Sweden visited that year, he awarded me a medal in appreciation of the hospitality he enjoyed. Although I have been invited to white tie events where the wearing of medals is expected, I have never had the courage to wear mine.

That same summer, the Democratic convention that nominated Jimmy Carter took place in New York City, and I was an alternate delegate. My daughter Amy had her first taste of politics working as a page for the Rhode Island delegation, a job she enjoyed very much. At the next convention, she was appointed to the security detail for the VIP section and she was in her glory with dozens of movie stars roaming the aisles.

That spring, Phyllis Wagner decided that it would be a nice idea to have a guide book to the city for the delegates coming to the convention. She asked me, Charlotte Ford, and Susan Fine (now Susan Burke) to work on the project. It turned out to be so time-consuming that we missed the convention, but managed to get it published the next year as a paperback titled, *Charlotte, Isabelle, Phyllis & Susan's NY, NY: A Woman's Guide to Shops, Services and Restaurants*. Phyllis's late husband, Bennett Cerf, had been chairman of Random

New York Harbor, 1976 (photo taken by the United States Coast Guard)

House, and they were our publishers. The book sold very well while we were promoting it on talk radio shows, but once our appearances stopped, the book sales slowly decreased. I still have copies at all my phones and sometimes refer to them instead of the telephone directory. One of the sad things is that New York changes so rapidly that guide books become inaccurate very quickly.

Another event that is clear in my memory during that bicentennial year was the parade of tall ships in New York Harbor. On the Fourth of July, the *USS Forrestal* was on the Hudson River for the occasion and it seemed that virtually the entire United States government was on board. Congressmen, senators, Supreme Court justices, and both the president and the vice president were all in attendance. Governor Carey was allotted quite a few spaces and after he made his selection of guests, I was one of those in charge of accepting or rejecting hundreds of requests for invitations. I must say that I was the most popular girl in New York during that process.

The day of the parade, I was designated to accompany Princess Grace of Monaco to the ship. With my friend, Dick Huber, a professor at Hunter College, I met her at a 23rd Street dock where we boarded a small boat and were taken to the *USS Forrestal*. She was very beautiful and very cordial. That part of the day's experience was pleasant, but didn't compare with the solemnity of seeing virtually our entire government assembled en masse. In the evening there was a splendid display of fireworks at Battery Park. Although we had been invited to several parties, Dick and I chose to go down to the Battery where we stood with millions of our fellow New Yorkers celebrating our country and our city. How sad it is for me to remember the great esteem the United States enjoyed at that time compared to the world's view of us today. Quel dommage.

It was Dick Huber who in 1978 asked me to teach an extension course at Hunter College called New York Women of Achievement. Each week I invited a distinguished woman

"I Love New York"
Political Life in New York City, 1970s-1995

to lecture and then answer questions, which I moderated. Some of the participants were Barbara Walters, former co-host of the *Today Show* and later the ubiquitous television interviewer; Bess Myerson, Commissioner of the New York City Department of Consumer Affairs; Grace Mirabella, editor of *Vogue* magazine; Charlotte Ford, who had a clothing company and had written, or was about to write, a book on etiquette; Elaine Kaufman, the doyen of Elaine's, the famous watering spot for authors; and Gillian Sorenson, the city's liaison to the UN diplomatic community and now Senior Advisor at the United Nations Foundation. We always had full attendance in the class which ran from 5:00 p.m. to 7:00 p.m. and was held at an auditorium on 55th Street. On the night Bess Myerson appeared, she wanted to continue long after the class ended. I was due at a Carey dinner, however, and was not about to be late, so I left her to speak as long as she wanted and asked that she dismiss the class. Bess and I were friends for many years, but later drifted apart, and I have not seen her for a long time.

The bicentennial celebrations were a welcome relief from the financial crises of the previous years. That year, a loan guarantee had been pending in Congress to help rescue the city from economic collapse. Governor Carey was committed to developing a fiscal plan that would rescue the city from insolvency. For that purpose, he oversaw the creation of the Municipal Assistance Corporation (informally known as "Big Mac") and the "I Love New York" campaign. What a success that turned out to be. I can remember Carey inviting me into his office while he called Mary Wells Lawrence, the well-respected advertising executive, asking her to devise a campaign to promote New York and increase the influx of tourists to our state. Because it was important to gain the support of the Congress for the loan guarantee, I suggested to the governor that he take his former congressional colleagues up to the Windows on the World restaurant at the top of the World Trade Center. Looking out at the magnificent spectacle of New York City, his colleagues would certainly want to help us. We arranged a reception there for the congressional members and other visiting dignitaries and it was very successful. I have always been convinced that the sight of our city from the top of the World Trade Center helped persuade them to vote *aye* on the loan guarantee.

Another function held at the Windows on the World was a luncheon that I arranged for the governor during the bicentennial celebration. The view at my table was particularly charming; sitting at my one side was the Spanish Ambassador to the United Nations, and on the other side, the United States Ambassador to Spain. On the opposite side of the table was actor Cary Grant and beyond him, my beloved city. Who could ask for anything more? I would often visit the World Trade Center during those years to dine at the wonderful restaurant and to attend meetings when Mario Cuomo was governor and had his office there. All of these associations made the September 11th disaster even more devastating for me.

As special assistant to Governor Carey, part of my responsibilities was to interact with any business or governmental visitors to the United States who wanted to learn about our system of government or how to go about doing business with our country. In late 1979, I wrote a memo to Governor Carey suggesting that the state of New York make a greater effort to export our products, particularly clothing, since the garment industry was one of our largest employers and the number of jobs in that field was declining. That suggestion led to one of the most fascinating projects of my career—The New York Fashion Market World Buyers Week, which was attended by buyers and journalists from all over the world.

We first organized a steering committee with members from the apparel industry, labor unions, the private sector, and the local and federal governments. A decision was then made to hold an international fashion fair in May of 1981 that we anticipated would stimulate U.S. apparel exports and highlight New York City as the fashion capital of the world.

I traveled to Washington and obtained a sizable grant from the United States Department of Commerce. We also had state funding and raised money from the manufacturers. Through an intensive promotional campaign abroad, we attracted several hundred foreign buyers to our city and presented the variety and quality of apparel manufactured in the United States, particularly that of New York. Marifé Hernandez accompanied me to Paris and to London to promote the program. Pan American World Airlines provided the transportation. We hosted an "I Love New York" booth at the Prêt à Porter Paris, along with hundreds of other booths representing manufacturers from all over the world. The French reacted to our presence in a typical way; we were given a poor location for our booth, and they gave us very little publicity. We then staged a fashion show at the American Embassy in Paris, and that event did attract more press. Fortunately, Hebe Dorsey, the number one French fashion journalist, was enthusiastic in her coverage of the event. Later, when Hebe came to New York, Eugenia Shepard suggested that I give a cocktail party, which I did with great pleasure. What I remember most clearly about that event is that I met Monsieur Marc, New York's best-known hairdresser. He asked if he could begin doing my hair and I became a client of his for many years.

In London, we invited buyers to tea and visited them in the larger stores. We met with representatives of the fashion industry and relied a good deal on the personal contacts we had developed with the fashion press. Also, thanks to the creative efforts of Lou Hammond, Pan American's head of public relations, we staged a fashion show for the passengers aboard our return flight to New York with flight attendants modeling our American designs.

The international fair ran from May 10-15, 1981. The Parsons School of Design provided the facilities for the event and George Trescher, a brilliant marketing expert, came up with an outstanding technological program to assist our guests. Computers were provided so that each participating company could show its line and arrange appointments for interested buyers. Any company wishing to participate had to pay an entry fee, and with the exception of Calvin Klein, I believe that virtually every important apparel company in New York was represented. At the closing event, Governor Carey gave a huge cocktail party at the Metropolitan Museum of Art where the Costume Institute was opened for viewing by the guests, and he graciously credited me with the success of the Fashion Fair.

The fair received excellent press coverage both in New York and abroad. Surprisingly, the only newspaper that showed little interest was the one that should have been the most involved, the *Women's Wear Daily*, a well-known fashion industry trade paper. That puzzled me because acting on the advice of Bill Blass I had given them advance information about the event and had tried to keep them completely informed for both their New York and Paris editions. I later learned that Michael Coady, then the editor, was upset because we had not contacted them when we advertised in Japan. We were not aware, however, that the paper had a Japanese office, which resulted in an unfortunate misunderstanding.

"I Love New York" booth at the Prêt à Porter Paris

We never assessed the actual dollar return on the World Buyers Week event, but I am certain that the buyers were impressed with both the technology of our set-up at Parsons

"I Love New York"
Political Life in New York City, 1970s-1995

and the vast array of clothing that New York manufacturers produced. Although the so-called "couture" designers lent prestige to the event, what Europe could not duplicate was the mass-produced quality fashion from the United States. A second buyers' week was later planned for November of 1981, but the dollar had risen so high, we knew we would be unable to attract the buyers, so the event never took place.

My work on the Fashion Fair brought me in close contact with all the great New York designers of the time, although I knew some of them socially before the event. My closest friend among the designers was Pauline Trigere, of whom I write about in more detail later. I also knew Bill Blass fairly well. There were times when Nancy Kissinger and I would order the same outfit from him, and I used to joke with her (as well as with Bill and his staff) that her dress always arrived long before my own did. People always told me I looked like Nancy, although the only resemblance I see is our six foot stature. One day, as Amy and I were shopping, a man approached us and said, "Good afternoon, Mrs. Kissinger. How are you today?" I answered that I was fine, but not Mrs. Kissinger. "That's all right," he said, "I won't tell anyone it's you."

I was also acquainted with Adolfo, Oscar de la Renta, Geoffrey Beene, and Mary McFadden. I had been a "private client" of theirs for quite some time—that's a euphemism for buying wholesale. My love affair with fashion and the knowledge I had acquired during the Fashion Fair did not go unnoticed. For the past twenty-five years, I have been one of the nominators for the International Best Dressed List.

In those days, there were many New York charitable events that drew fashion-minded guests, myself included. Occasionally, many of us showed up adorned in the same designer dress or suit. We were all nonchalant about it, of course, and enjoyed seeing the varied ways each of us interpreted the same design. At one benefit for the Casita Maria settlement house, six women wore similar Adolfo gowns with ribbon stripes that complemented the event's Latin theme. There were also several separate Adolfo events where a group of us showed up wearing identical bowed suits. *Women's Wear Daily* loved to photograph duplicates like that. Of course, this made the designers very happy, but I was never pleased to be represented as so unoriginal in my selections.

Adolfo is a very sweet, thoughtful gentleman. In his showroom on 57th Street, there was a beautiful paper-mache sunburst, which I admired every time I visited there. When he was closing his business, he called and said, "I would like you to have the sunburst," and he sent it over. It now hangs in the living room of my Florida home.

An Adolfo event at the Plaza
(courtesy of New York Times photographer, Bill Cunningham)

Working for Governor Carey was very rewarding and I was particularly honored when he issued a proclamation from the state designating December 5, 1979 as Isabelle Leeds Day. Carey read the proclamation at a surprise birthday party that my friends threw for me at Orsini's.

Many believed that Hugh Carey was on the road to becoming a viable candidate for the presidency, but fate had other plans. Carey was an outstanding governor and is credited with saving New York City from bankruptcy by overseeing the

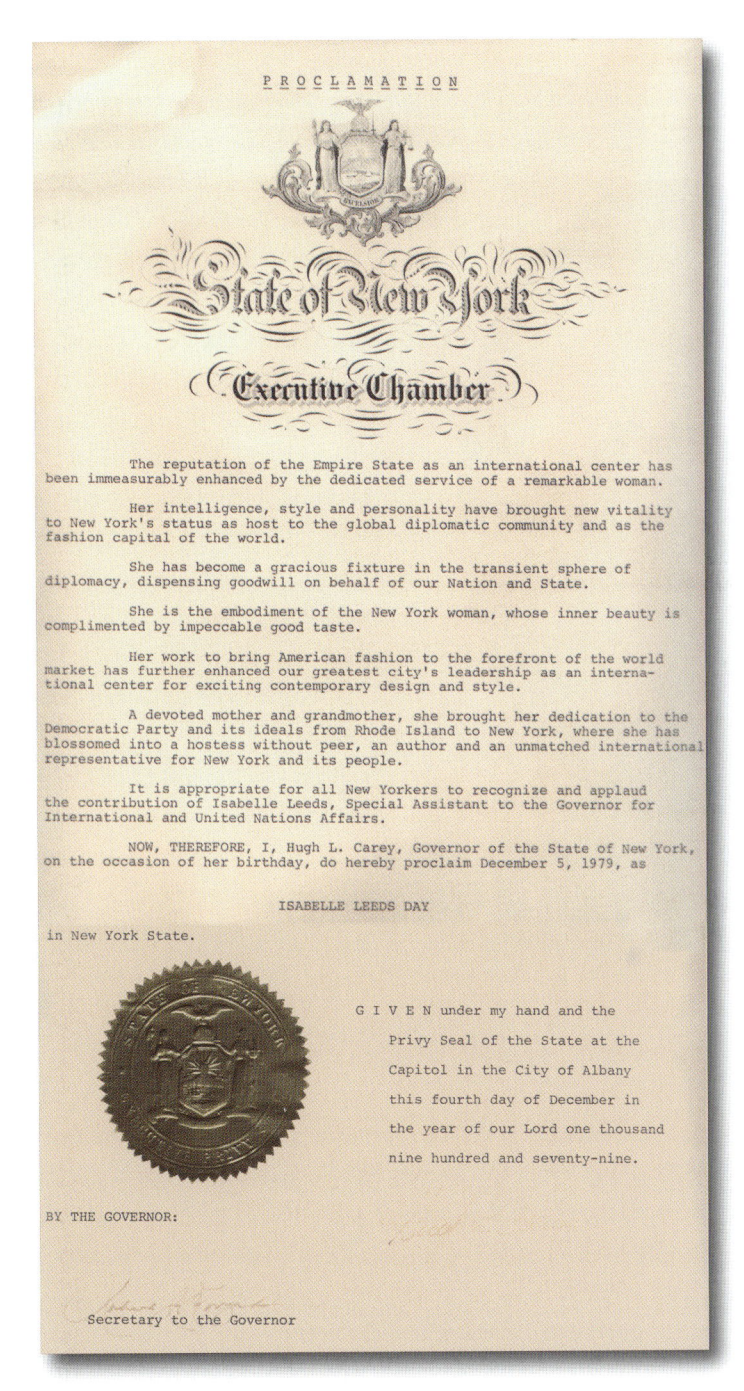

"I Love New York"
Political Life in New York City, 1970s-1995

> **PROCLAMATION**
>
> **State of New York**
>
> **Executive Chamber**
>
> The reputation of the Empire State as an international center has been immeasurably enhanced by the dedicated service of a remarkable woman.
>
> Her intelligence, style and personality have brought new vitality to New York's status as host to the global diplomatic community and as the fashion capital of the world.
>
> She has become a gracious fixture in the transient sphere of diplomacy, dispensing goodwill on behalf of our Nation and State.
>
> She is the embodiment of the New York woman, whose inner beauty is complimented by impeccable good taste.
>
> Her work to bring American fashion to the forefront of the world market has further enhanced our greatest city's leadership as an international center for exciting contemporary design and style.
>
> A devoted mother and grandmother, she brought her dedication to the Democratic Party and its ideals from Rhode Island to New York, where she has blossomed into a hostess without peer, an author and an unmatched international representative for New York and its people.
>
> It is appropriate for all New Yorkers to recognize and applaud the contribution of Isabelle Leeds, Special Assistant to the Governor for International and United Nations Affairs.
>
> NOW, THEREFORE, I, Hugh L. Carey, Governor of the State of New York, on the occasion of her birthday, do hereby proclaim December 5, 1979, as
>
> ISABELLE LEEDS DAY
>
> in New York State.
>
> G I V E N under my hand and the Privy Seal of the State at the Capitol in the City of Albany this fourth day of December in the year of our Lord one thousand nine hundred and seventy-nine.
>
> BY THE GOVERNOR:
>
> Secretary to the Governor

establishment of the Municipal Assistance Corporation and establishing other policies to make the city fiscally responsible. With Kevin Cahill, he worked with the state's medical establishment to improve health services for all New Yorkers, including the mentally disabled. Carey had a talent for picking top-notch people to whom he then gave the necessary leeway to act, among them Kevin Cahill; Commerce Commissioner, Bill Hassett, who made giant strides in improving the state's business climate; David Burke, a former aide to Ted Kennedy, who was Carey's number one assistant; Judah Gribetz, counselor to the Governor; Peter Goldmark, the state budget director and later executive director of the Metropolitan Transportation Authority; Dick Ravitch, chair of the Urban Development Corporation; Orin Lehman, commissioner of Parks and Recreation; and Mike del Giudice, deputy chief of staff to the governor. All were enormously talented men who contributed to the success of the Carey administration and made it such a pleasure to be associated with the governor's office.

With Governor Mario Cuomo

When Carey ran for reelection in 1978, Mario Cuomo, who had served as secretary of state in his first administration, ran as lieutenant governor. In both positions, his office was in the same suite as the governor's office. During this time, I developed a great respect and admiration for him. One Sunday in the late 1970s, while on my way home from the Golden Door spa in California, Mario was traveling on the same plane as I. When we landed at JFK, he asked how I was getting home. I told him I would get a porter who would get me a taxi. "No, no," said the Lieutenant Governor, "You just wait here for a minute." Off he went with his luggage and within five minutes reappeared, took both of my large suitcases in hand (I have never learned to travel light), and escorted me out to the sidewalk where he helped me into a cab and then went on his way. That told me a lot about the kind of person he was. A few years later, when he was running for governor of New York and called to ask for my support, I replied that I could never refuse him after he had been so nice to me at the airport. He thought I should have better reasons to think he would be a good governor and indeed I did. We have remained good friends to this day. My son David became a great friend and supporter of Mario's son Andrew who is now the Attorney General of New York State.

"I Love New York"
Political Life in New York City, 1970s-1995

In the early 1980s, when I started spending more time away from New York, my political activities waned. Although I remained friendly with Governor Cuomo and his fabulous wife Matilda, who started a major mentoring program in the United States, among many other successful service projects, I did not take a job in his administration. Mario did appoint me to the United Nations Development Corporation and to the Christopher Columbus Commission, two-term appointments that were very interesting. By this time, however, I had been involved in politics and government for more than twenty years and I felt that was enough.

WMCA RADIO

7

Toward the end of the Carey Administration, my friend, Ellen Strauss, inquired about what I was going to do next. When I said I had no idea, she asked me to join her and her husband Peter at their radio station, WMCA, as director of public affairs. Thus began a few great years with them, writing editorials on current issues and reporting on fashion shows (I found there was a huge difference in how you watched a show as a reporter and how you observed as a buyer). I gave a weekly report called "Leeds on Living," which covered a myriad of topics often drawn from my own life experiences and observations. I once tried to have the reports published as a book, but never pursued it past the first turndown.

I also produced and was occasionally a guest host for the Barry Gray Talk Show, which emanated from Elaine's Restaurant at noon every week. My involvement with the Barry Gray show was a great learning experience. As producer, I had to round up a good mix of guests to make a lively show. We had show business celebrities, politicians, businessmen, educators, doctors, and anyone else who I thought would provide interesting conversation. For example, I once noticed that one of the women's magazines had something called a Royalty Editor, so I asked him to be a guest. Of course, all of these people had very busy schedules and coordinating their appearances was a time-consuming job. The work of a host is even more difficult. I had to do extensive research on every guest and prepare a list of questions that might elicit interesting answers. Hours of work were involved. The first time I guest-hosted, Marifé Hernandez was scheduled to be my guest, speaking about her role as chief of protocol at the UN. She got caught in traffic, however, and appeared at the studio ten minutes after the show went on the air. Ellen Strauss and I had to engage in chitchat for ten minutes, which to me seemed like an eternity. I have never thought of myself as a great conversationalist and those ten minutes really put me to the test.

Ellen was a very active, involved person and I joined her in several outside projects. In the early 1980s, she arranged for my appointment to the board of the Partnership for New York City, an organization comprised of CEOs from many of New York's greatest companies. This association enabled me to organize and fund a program that would bring together teenagers and senior citizens. The idea was for the teenagers to run errands, go shopping, or just provide company, while the seniors would help with homework and more importantly, give the youngsters the benefit of their life experiences. Although this pilot program took place in what was not the best of neighborhoods, the problems that arose were not with the youths, but with the seniors who could not seem to trust the young people despite the presence of the police and clergy. The program wasn't as successful as I would have liked, but it was a worthwhile effort. At the time, the Partnership was run by a talented woman named Kathryn Wylde. Over twenty years later, Kathy is still bringing her leadership skills to bear on that organization with great success.

Leeds on Living

ALTERNATE UNITED STATES REPRESENTATIVE TO THE UNITED NATIONS

8

Isabelle and Bill Clinton at Tavern on the Green (© Photograph by Robert A. Cumins)

I first met Bill Clinton in late 1991 and was bowled over by him, along with most of the people gathered that day at the home of Kathy Rayner, daughter of Anne Cox Chambers, former Ambassador to Belgium. He immediately became my candidate for president and commencing early the next year, I began doing something I had never done for a candidate before—actively fundraising. During the months preceding the election I was able to raise nearly five hundred thousand dollars for his campaign, and for me that was a significant amount. As a result, and with a strong endorsement from Senator Pell, President Clinton appointed me Alternate United States Representative to the United Nations for the session beginning September 1994. Earlier that year, my good friend and well-known astrologer, Arlene Dahl, had predicted that I would receive a very important international appointment. Makes one wonder, doesn't it?

My office at the United States Mission to the UN was located on First Avenue and 45th Street, directly across the street from the UN. Each morning at 8:30 a.m., I would arrive, go through security, and proceed to my office on an upper floor. Once a week we had the privilege of attending a staff meeting presided over by the U.S. Representative to the UN, Madeleine Albright. What an outstanding woman she is. Not only does she possess great brilliance, but she has a sense of humor to match. How fascinating it was to get a first-hand insider's report on the international doings of the previous week.

There were three alternate representatives and our duties were varied. Sometimes we were assigned to sit in and report on different committee meetings, and other times we were asked to monitor the proceedings of the General Assembly sessions. During those sessions, there was a great deal of action in the aisles as the delegates discussed the various issues. Our main task was to convince other members to agree with the American position. It was a matter of great exhilaration when we could convince other delegates to vote

Alternate United States Representative to the United Nations

with us. This lobbying effort took place not only on the floor of the UN, but at the many dinners and receptions we had to attend in order to develop relationships with the representatives from other nations. In that sense, the United Nations is very similar to Washington, in that differences of opinion can often be resolved by informal conversations at social gatherings. My good friend, Ambassador Enriquillo del Rosario (now married to the former Audrey Zauderer and still an active participant at the Dominican Republic's UN Mission), was of enormous assistance in helping me acclimate to the operations of the United Nations.

At one point, I was asked to deliver a speech to the General Assembly that had been written at the State Department. As a former speechwriter, I found certain lines that were not to my liking, so I changed them. I was told, however, that every word uttered had to be cleared, so back to Washington it went. I think my corrections were accepted because they did not change the meaning of the remarks. I have a video clip of that address. Another time I was allowed to sit in the U.S. Ambassador's seat and do the actual voting. That vote had to do with the issue of equating Zionism with racism and our vote was *nay*. Although we were in the minority, it was thrilling to cast the vote for my country.

U.S. Mission to the U.N.

ISABELLE R. LEEDS
U.S. Alternate Representative to the
49th United Nations General Assembly

799 United Nations Plaza
New York, NY 10017

Tel: (212) 415-4489
Fax: (212) 415-4162

Alternate United States
Representative to the United Nations

*Alternate U.S. Representative to UN with Amy, Governor Carey,
and U.S. Representative to the UN, Madeleine Albright*

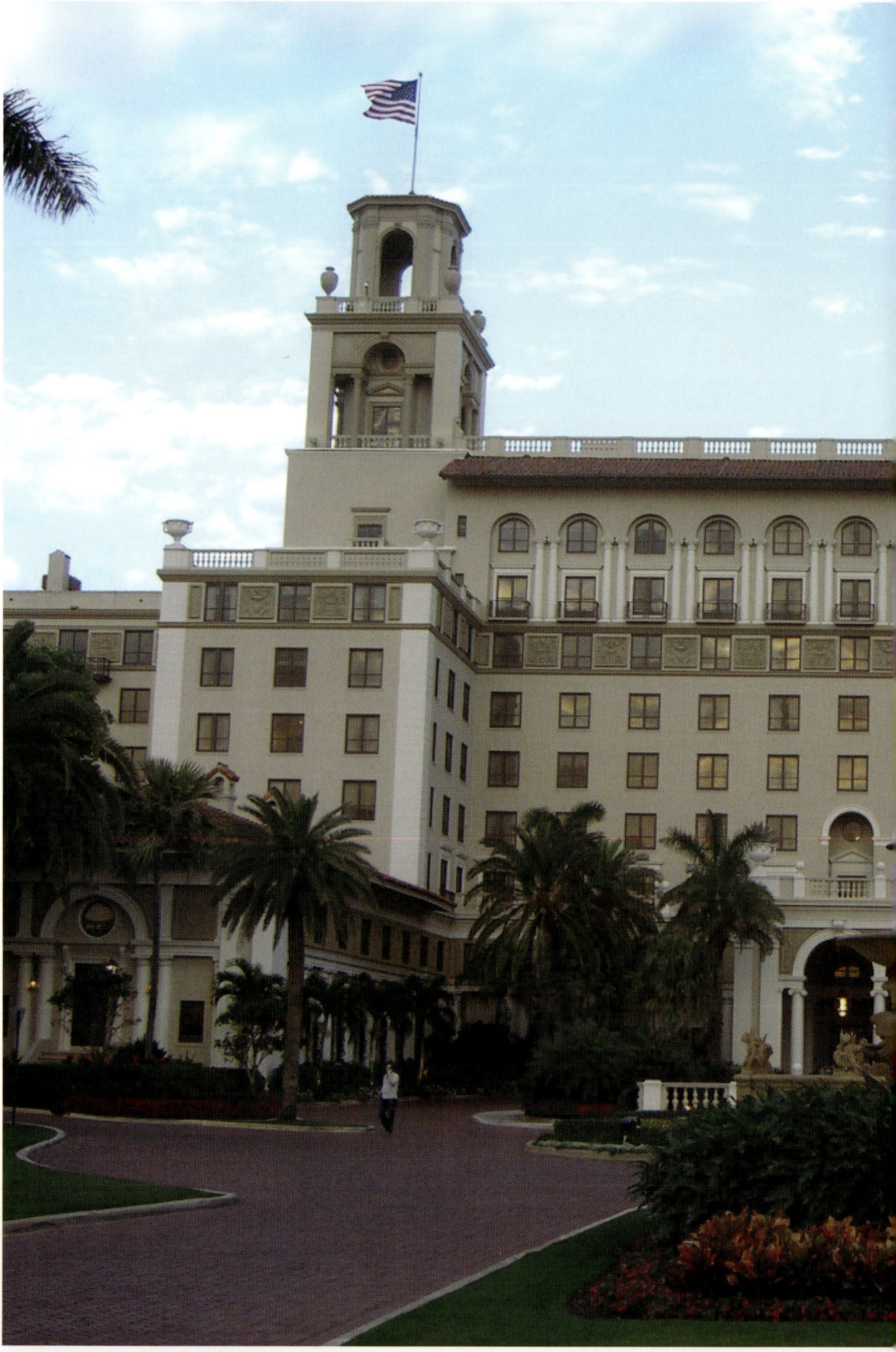

PALM BEACH AND RETIREMENT

9

By the early 1980s, I finally decided that I could no longer deal with the snow and ice of a New York winter, so began a new chapter in my life, that of a part-time Floridian. I began spending more and more time there and eventually I became a resident of Palm Beach in 2003. My first apartment came about as the result of a coincidence. As I was having my hair done one afternoon, I began to chat with the woman in the next chair. I mentioned that I was about to start looking for a furnished apartment and she said, "I am selling my place furnished. Would you like to see it?" When we were finished with our beauty treatments, we went over to her building and I bought her apartment on the spot. I spent four happy years there and then decided I needed a little more space so I purchased an apartment right across the street where I have been ensconced happily ever since.

One of the first things I did after moving to Palm Beach was to join the Breakers Golf Club. It is not a very good course, but it was convenient and I made good use of it for several years. The final year I was at my first flat, an old friend, Jerry Tishman, visited for a few weeks. After I moved to a larger space, he started spending most of the winter there with me. He did his own thing during the day and I did mine. In the evenings, we would go out together. During my first few years in Florida, I also spent time with my Providence pals, Lorraine and Heinz Silberthau, and Ruth and Leo Marks; both had homes at a nearby golfing community. We exchanged visits fairly often for golf and for dinner. A few years later, they moved back to Rhode Island, and I really hated to see them leave.

In 1991, the Palm Beach Country Club finally dropped its long-held prejudice against single women members, and Carol

Palm Beach and Retirement

Feinberg, Estelle Gelman, and I became the first women admitted on our own behalf without the marriage requirement. I had been told at one point that "we have too many women members and they will not want to spend money on all the things we might want to do." I should have replied that the women members whose husbands had died were considered non-voting members and couldn't have voted for expenditures anyway. I had many friends lobbying on my behalf, but I'm not sure what made the board change its mind. In the end, I guess saner and probably younger heads prevailed, or perhaps, there were other reasons that might have been political in nature.

Being denied the opportunity to join the club of my choice was not my first encounter with gender discrimination. A few months after I left Rhode Island and moved into my apartment in New York City, my decorator, Charles Dear, who by this time had become a good friend, told me that he knew a man, Bernie Ruggieri, who had recently been named chairman of the New York City Democratic Committee. He offered to introduce us and I quickly agreed. Bernie called and offered me a job as his administrative assistant, an offer I accepted with alacrity. To discuss the position, we set up a lunch meeting at an eating club in the Waldorf-Astoria. Since I am always early, I arrived before he did and immediately sensed that I was the subject of curious glances; however, I put that down to the fact that I was unknown there. When Bernie arrived, he approached the front desk and returned to me crimson-faced—it seemed that the club was for men only. We adjourned to another dining room and had a pleasant lunch, during which he explained my duties. At least, I had gained a new title and a new friend.

Following my term as alternate representative to the UN in 1994, and after a great deal of discomfort, I finally

Palm Beach and Retirement

succumbed to the dreaded knee replacement. It is a very unpleasant operation and the recuperation is perhaps even more agonizing. The surgery took place at the Hospital for Special Surgery and was performed by Dr. Russell Warren who at that time was chief of the orthopedic department. He was also the team doctor for the New York Giants football team, of which my friend, Bob Tisch, was half-owner. I asked Bob to please tell Dr. Warren that he must fix my knee as if I were going to play on the football team. I was never offered a spot with the Giants, but my knee did show a great improvement after the surgery. After months of intense therapy, I was able to return to Palm Beach and began playing golf almost immediately. I am quite disciplined, and to this day, I use my recumbent bicycle every single day, but I am not nearly as spry as I once was.

In addition to my knee replacement, I had to undergo another type of surgery in 1999. On a routine visit to the dermatologist, a small spot was removed from my left leg, and three days later I was called with the terrible news that it was a melanoma. Shortly thereafter, I had surgery at Memorial Sloan-Kettering, convalesced, then had my lymph nodes tested, which resulted in further surgery to remove them. Although I did have a good recovery, I was left with lymphedema, which causes a swelling of the leg. Since that day, I have never worn skirts, only pantsuits. If that is the worst problem that arises from that trauma, I shall settle happily, but it is of great importance to me that my descendants visit a dermatologist regularly.

At one point over the years, I seemed to be accident-prone and suffered several injuries. Twice I fell in my apartment, one time with no injury and the other time breaking my nose, as well as a front tooth. In 2004, I tripped over something on the floor at Bloomingdale's and broke my shoulder. That also required sustained therapy, most of which I did at a wonderful institution, the Rehabilitation Center for Children and Adults in Palm Beach. At the time of my accident, my friends said it happened because I was in Bloomingdale's instead of

Bergdorf's. Actually, I was not even shopping but walking through the store merely as a shortcut to Third Avenue.

Another injury occurred while I was visiting Paris with my son David. After a few great days, we were getting ready to leave for Florence to meet David's wife, Kathy, and her mother, but that was not to be. When I returned to the room to take my bath that last afternoon, I found my leg covered with blood. It did not hurt and I had no recollection of bumping into anything, but there was a huge gash. As we tried to stop the bleeding, we called the physician who was on call at the Hotel Crillon. He finally arrived, butterflied the wound, and said I could continue on my trip, but to take it easy. To confirm that judgment, I called my physician in New York who cautioned, "That is not a good idea. Your injury is on the leg that had a knee replacement and if you ever get an infection you will be in real trouble." So back I flew to New York the next day with David who insisted on accompanying me. I saw a plastic surgeon who treated the wound and said that we would hope for the best. The best never happened and I had to have a skin graft to heal the problem.

Life in Palm Beach is a full-time occupation. I think of it as an overnight camp for adults. At camp, you take a lot of lessons and learn a lot of sports; and at the clubs in Florida, you take bridge, golf, tennis, yoga, or exercise lessons. At camp, you take arts and crafts classes; in Palm Beach you collect art. When I'm in Florida, I play a lot of golf, a lot of bridge, take Pilates, and sometimes have physical therapy. I also attend a lot of parties (some things never change). It is strange to recall that there was a time when I would say, "Five days in Palm Beach is all I can deal with." Today, it is my home; I spend about six months there and I am never quite ready to leave. My primary activity is golf, but one year when I sustained a stress fracture in my leg, I managed to keep busy

Palm Beach and Retirement

for a month without golf and concentrated instead on bridge and books. I have always been a voracious reader and usually go through at least two books a week. Although I prefer biographies, I also read a lot of spy stories and novels of political intrigue.

Somehow, I always think of life in Palm Beach as stress-free living. It is less hectic, easier to get around, and more relaxed than New York, which by the way, I shall never stop adoring. It has only recently occurred to me that one of the reasons I find Palm Beach so stress-free is the fact that as I have aged, I have learned not to worry about the small things.

SOCIAL GATHERINGS AND PHILANTHROPY
10

On the town

It has probably become apparent that in both my political life and my personal life, parties have always played a large role. I don't deny it. I have always loved people and enjoyed social gatherings, both giving them and going to them. Some of the best parties I ever attended were those given by my friends, Josh and Nedda Logan. Josh was a very successful Broadway director and Nedda had formerly been a singer. At their River House home they often invited various songwriters who would sit down at the piano after dinner and play many of the tunes they had written. What fun it was to sing along. Then, as now, I knew every word and only one note.

I have also enjoyed many wonderful parties at the home of my good friend, Audrey Zauderer (now Audrey del Rosario) at her homes in New York, Bedford, Southampton, and in Round Hill, Jamaica. She was, in fact, known as the "Queen of Round Hill" for many years, and I often visited there with her and her late husband, George. I first met Audrey shortly after I moved to New York. I was attending a charity auction and she was seated beside me, both of us wearing the same Bill Blass outfit. Mine now resides in the Costume Institute at the Metropolitan Museum of Art and hers is still in her closet. We became almost instant friends. A few years after George died, Audrey married Enriquillo del Rosario, ambassador from the Dominican Republic to the United Nations. She sold her Jamaican property and began wintering in Palm Beach, Florida, where she continues her entertaining ways.

Marylou Whitney is another fabulous hostess, giving giant galas in Saratoga Springs to open the racing season and in Louisville for the Kentucky

Ambassador Enriquillo & Audrey del Rosario
(photo printed with permission of Lucien Capehart Photography)

Social Gatherings and Philanthropy

Derby, as well as hosting parties at her beautiful homes on Fifth Avenue and in Palm Beach. She has since sold the latter two. Marylou is one of the most dynamic women I have ever known and a bundle of great personality and fun.

Although she was known as the "queen of mean," the late Leona Helmsley and her husband, Harry, hosted some of the greatest parties in New York. They owned the Park Lane Hotel and resided in a penthouse atop the building. To celebrate Harry's birthday each year, Leona gave an "I'm Just Wild About Harry" party. Cocktails were held around the olympic size swimming pool and caviar, fois gras, dozens of delicious hot and cold hors d'oeuvres, and champagne were served in abundance. The party would then adjourn to the ballroom of the hotel for dinner and dancing. Each year there was a different party favor given; one year, it was large campaign button that said, "I'm Just Wild About Harry" (and Harry wore a pin that said, "I'm Harry"). Other years it was a music box playing that same song title, an inscribed t-shirt, and on and on. After a few of Harry's events, Leona decided to celebrate her own birthday at their estate in Greenwich. This, too, was extravagant in its abundance. At one of those parties, my daughter and son-in-law were also in attendance. Amy and I were chatting with a very prominent dermatologist and I commented on how pretty Amy looked. The dermatologist's immediate response to me was "I can make you look just like that, call me on Monday." That was when the craze for cosmetic injections was becoming popular. It was one call I never made.

There were two dinner parties that I shall never forget. The first was a dinner in which I was seated between Leonard Bernstein and Mayor Ed Koch. I had met the composer, but did not know him well. I had often been in Koch's company and knew him to be a loquacious guest, but not that evening. Not only did the conversation go directly over my head, but even the voluble Ed Koch was unable to get a word in during Bernstein's monologue. Then there was the evening that Governor Carey gave a very large formal dinner at the

Social Gatherings And Philanthropy

executive mansion in Albany. When he rose to give his toast, the first thing he said was "If you don't like where you are sitting, don't blame me because Isabelle Leeds arranged the seating." That was thirty years ago and every time I see Leonard Lauder, the eldest son of Estée Lauder, he repeats that comment to anyone who is standing nearby.

In the 1970s and 1980s, there were several grandes dames in New York City with whom I was acquainted. First and foremost was Brooke Astor. I knew her only casually, but one evening when I was seated across from her at a dinner party, I was entranced with the beautiful pearls she was wearing and thought to myself that my brand new South Sea pearl necklace paled in comparison. She happened to give me a ride home that evening and the first thing she said to me was, "How you do like my fake Yves Saint Laurent pearls?" proving that beauty is indeed in the eyes of the beholder.

Two leading hostesses and close friends of mine were Mildred Hilson and Jean Stralem. I must confess that it was from Mildred that I first learned the practice of going around the table and saying something about each of the guests. Her favorite cause was the Hospital for Special Surgery and under her leadership it became one of New York City's best attended charities. For Mildred's ninetieth birthday, she gave a beautiful party at the roof of the St. Regis Hotel. Hubert de Givenchy made her gown, delivered it personally, and attended the event at which Richard Nixon sat down at the piano and played Happy Birthday. Someone also gave her a ten-year subscription to *New York* magazine, which I thought was a very clever gift. Jean Stralem was someone who gave a dinner every week in her lovely Park Avenue apartment. She was also one of the first great art collectors that I knew. The first time I was invited to one of her gatherings, she asked me to sit down beside her on the couch. Across the room was one of the most beautiful and one of the most famous Matisse paintings. From then on, I always sat on the couch looking at that beautiful work of art. One evening, the couch was full so I sat down in front of the fireplace and there over the couch was another version of that fabulous Matisse. The apartment was full of wonderful impressionist paintings. It was a joy to be a guest in her home.

Another world class hostess was Estée Lauder. Her dinners were extremely formal and each guest was served by an individual butler. Estée was known for her frankness and one night she said to me, "You look so fabulous tonight, you don't look a bit like Isabelle Leeds." I was not insulted because I knew she meant it as a great compliment. As much as I enjoyed all the parties, I did realize that my social popularity was in good part related to my political prominence. Nonetheless, I had some wonderful times with some very special people.

I have hosted many parties of my own at my apartment, including three or four dinner dances. Each time, all the furniture was removed from the living room, library, and adjoining guest room. Cocktails and hors d'oeuvres were served in the two adjoining rooms, and then guests proceeded into the living room where six tables of ten had been placed around a dance floor. I have often been asked to reinstate those parties, but I feel those days are better as fond memories.

One short-lived series of gatherings I enjoyed hosting was called "Cocktails and Conversation." Ellen Straus, the head of WMCA Radio, and I would invite two well-known personalities with two totally different approaches or ideologies to lead the evening's conversation. The idea was to get diverse groups together. One night, we asked David Rockefeller and Benjamin Hooks, head of the NAACP (who recently was awarded the Medal of Freedom by President George Bush), to speak. David Rockefeller probably had a greater influence on the affairs of our country, at least in the economic realm, than his brother Nelson who was governor of New York and vice president of the United States. I have always felt that David was like a fourth branch of government, because almost every major foreign leader who came to New York made an immediate appointment to see him. The conversation at these gatherings was always lively

Social Gatherings And Philanthropy

and I even remember having a short mail correspondence with Alan Greenspan about some of the topics we had discussed at one of them.

On another occasion, I was asked by Esther Coopersmith, the veteran Washington fundraiser, if I would entertain the wives of those foreign ministers who were gathered at the UN in New York. I hosted a luncheon at my home and we arranged for Saks Fifth Avenue to stage a fashion show. The visitors were delighted, commenting that this was the first time such an event had been held in their honor.

In 1991, I hosted one of the first large fundraisers for Hillary Clinton's campaign for senator of New York. There were about one hundred people present, and every single guest was extremely impressed with her intelligence and charm. She was warm and friendly to my daughter and grandchildren, she spoke with the kitchen staff, asked for a tour of the apartment, and in general, was gracious to everyone with whom she spoke. It is easy for me to understand how people may not agree with all of her views, but it is difficult for me to fathom why some should dislike her so strongly.

In addition to being a party person, I must also admit to having always been a bit of a clothesaholic. On my first

From left - my granddaughter Stephanie, Amy, my grandson, Matthew, and Hillary Clinton

Christmas vacation from college, I told my father that many of the girls had a clothing allowance and I would like to have one as well. That was fine with him and I believe the amount we settled on was $100 a month. After the first of the year, I went shopping and spent my January, February, and March allowances on a few dresses. That left nothing for coats, shoes, stockings, purses and the like. It became immediately clear to me that this was not a good system, so that was the end of the clothing allowance.

I believe I inherited my love of clothes from my father. Because my mother was incapacitated, I often went shopping with my Aunt Rose, who had the same clothes gene that her brother possessed. She used to tell me it was more important to have a few quality pieces rather than a larger number of lesser quality things. I learned the quality part, but "few" was a word that was never in my vocabulary. It seems that I passed my addiction on to my children who in turn passed it on to their children. I have often told my granddaughter Stephanie that she is a fourth generation clothes junkie, and my grandsons are the same. Strange the things that can be inherited. Or was it environmental? My love of clothes is such that twice, while I was between projects, I thought of becoming a personal shopper. Every designer with whom I discussed this, however, thought it was a bad idea and warned that I could never deal with the foibles of the woman customer.

I am afraid that another thing my children have inherited is my dislike of flying. On my very first flight from Boston to New York, it was a stormy afternoon, so I stepped into the cockpit and asked the pilot, "Will you please fly extra carefully?" We landed safely and I have repeated that request every time I set foot into an airplane, to the great embarrassment of my traveling companions. Both Amy and David admit that they hate flying, but they do a lot of it anyway. My children also inherited the Russek characteristic of always being early, although I fear that Amy's European husband has changed her adherence to that rule. I have

Social Gatherings And Philanthropy

always thought it was extremely rude to keep people waiting, so it is one of the few sins of which I have never been guilty. Consequently, I spend a good deal of time waiting for others.

Along with my political career and busy social life, I was always very active in the community and served on quite a few boards. My major charitable connection for many years was with the March of Dimes. As a schoolgirl, I remember contributing dimes to the organization, so when I was asked to become a director in 1982, I eagerly accepted. The original mission of the group was to stamp out polio, and I believe it was the only disease-related campaign that has ever succeeded. What too few people realize is that the March of Dime's present goal is to eradicate birth defects. I was involved for many years in trying to educate the public about that goal and how to achieve it. I first served as the organization's vice chairman and later as chairman of the board of the New York Chapter. It was the March of Dimes that first sponsored the walk-a-thon, which has become such a

Getting ready for a party at my home in Greenwich

Halloween Party at Pat Lawford's (always ready for a photo; I was smiling under my mask)

successful fundraising mechanism that it has been copied by innumerable organizations, most notably in the AIDS Walk and Susan Komen's Race for the Cure. It is ironic to recall that although I have had the honor of attending White House dinners and other functions quite a few times, the only time I was actually in the Oval Office was on a March of Dimes visit during Ronald Reagan's presidency. I must say that regardless of one's background or how many times one does it, walking into the White House is a thrilling experience.

During the 1980s and early 1990s, I served on the board of the National Symphony Orchestra, which is headquartered in Washington D.C. That organization does a wonderful job of providing outreach programs to local school children, as well as offering an array of performances throughout the year. The one great fringe benefit of serving on the board was the annual invitation to attend the Kennedy Center Honors gala. There are events arranged around the gala, so it was always a wonderful weekend. During those years, I was also a board member of the Educational Foundation for the Fashion Industries at the Fashion Institute in New York.

I have always supported Jewish organizations, especially the group that began as the United Jewish Appeal (UJA), and which later merged with local Jewish groups all over the country to form federations of Jewish philanthropies. Approximately one half of every gift given goes to Israel and the other half is allocated to local organizations. I can remember back to the late 1950s when the Women's Division first held a meeting in Providence and the minimum gift for that Pacesetter Luncheon was $365. Today that division is called the Lion of Judah and the minimum gift is $5000. There are different categories of giving that go up incrementally to ever higher levels. When one becomes a Lion of Judah, a pin is presented and a different precious stone is given for each stage of giving.

In 1974, my friend Sylvia Hassenfeld was national chairman of the Women's Division of the UJA. She persuaded the governing body to allow women to participate for the first time in one of the groups' missions to Israel and asked me, Harriet Zimmerman (then Altschul), and a beautiful older (at least then she seemed older) woman named Biddie Kramer to accompany her. Despite my dislike of airplanes, especially on long trips, I agreed and had a wonderful experience. It was so exciting to see the wondrous accomplishments of the Jewish people, including the operation of the Hadassah Hospital (which my mother had strongly supported over the years), the trees that had been planted through the nickels and dimes of the Jewish National Fund (an organization with which my maternal grandfather had been associated), and the kibbutz at Kiryat Shmona. Flying over the Golan Heights, one could see how Israel would be loath to surrender that territory. Every moment was a thrilling experience. It was an added bonus to spend time with Sylvia. She is one of the outstanding women in American Jewish life. In addition to having served as national chairman of the UJA's Women Division, she has been president and

My friend, the remarkable Sylvia Hassenfeld

chairman of the American Jewish Joint Distribution Committee, vice-president of Brandeis University, and an officer in many other organizations. She currently serves on the board of the New York University Medical Center. She is charming, brilliant and beautiful, and possesses incredible energy. When we walk together she is always five feet in front of me. She constantly travels and is eager for every new experience. Sylvia is a truly remarkable woman and a warm, generous, loyal, and caring person whose friendship I cherish. We spend so much time together that we are frequently called by the other's name and answer to both.

A few years after that trip, I chaired a benefit for Lenox Hill Hospital in 1977, at which Jacqueline Kennedy Onassis was honorary chairman. At one planning meeting held at my home, Jackie was greeted at the door by my daughter Amy to whom she said "You should always wear red, it is so becoming on you." To his day, Amy's wardrobe contains a lot of that color. Also on the planning committee was Steve Ross, chairman of Warner Communications, now Time Warner, and one of the most generous men in the world. The proceeds went to his friend, Dr. James Nicholas, who had founded the Nicholas Institute of Sports Medicine and Athletic Trauma at Lenox Hill Hospital a few years earlier. Our star attractions for the benefit were Frank Sinatra and Robert Merrill who performed at Carnegie Hall, with Walter Cronkite as master of ceremonies. The former first lady and I both gave a short greeting on that famous stage (along with drawing a winning raffle ticket), and I must say I was even more nervous than the time I made my piano debut at the Starlight Roof. That evening, I disproved the old adage that the only way to get to Carnegie Hall is practice, practice, practice. The concert was followed by a dinner at the Waldorf-Astoria and the event was so well attended that we had to have two venues for the dinner. Warner Communications arranged for flashing neon signs to be made for the two rooms that were renamed for the occasion; the Empire Room became Frank's Place and the Wedgewood Room, Ol' Blue Eyes. Dinner chairman, Phyllis

Social Gatherings And Philanthropy

With Frank Sinatra (©Bill Mark)

Wagner, with her inimitable ingenuity, planned a typical Italian dinner with olives, large salamis, and bread, all spread out on tables covered by red-checked tablecloths and ready for the guests to nosh on as soon as they arrived from the concert. I had a great decision to make that evening—where to sit. My father was coming with a friend of his and Bill Hill and I could either sit with them or sit at Frank's table. Guess which one I chose? Wrong! My father always came first.

When I became involved with the March of Dimes, the chairman of the national board was Beverly Sills. Our friendship began on the basis of our mutual interest in the organization, but then it grew far beyond that and we became extremely close friends (she always called me part of her family).

One year, my son David had rented a summer house quite near the home of Beverly and her husband, Peter Greenough, on Martha's Vineyard. David's son, Nick, who was about three years old at the time, had developed a fear of the water and had to be lured into a pool. It was in Beverly and Peter's pool that he first found the joy of swimming. In later years, I stayed there with them and was always treated to a wonderful weekend. Back in New York, we lunched together, dined together, and for some years had a fairly regular bridge game in addition to sharing many family evenings together. Beverly took up the game of bridge only because Peter loved it and she played about as well as I sang. Also, each year on my birthday she would call and sing "Happy Birthday." Not only was she America's most beloved soprano, Beverly was also one of the most desired board members in the country. She was a woman of tremendous warmth, charm, wit, and intelligence, and contributed enormously to the many boards on which she served. As chairman of the board of the New York City Opera she propelled that group to a position as one of our country's finest opera companies. During her tenure as chairwoman of Lincoln Center, she raised millions of dollars and contributed invaluable service to that great organization. Despite her busy career and all of her outside interests she was always the most devoted wife and mother. When Peter had to enter a nursing home, for more than one year she visited with him every single morning for several hours. And she devoted almost all of her time in these last few years to her daughter Muffy, who had developed multiple sclerosis, and to raising money for research in that field. I have lost many friends over the past few years and I miss them all, but no one as much as I miss Beverly. I am still having difficulty coping with the loss. It was a real privilege to be her friend and I am grateful for our long friendship. I shall never forget her.

Social Gatherings And Philanthropy 127

Beverly Sills and Isabelle at a March of Dimes event

GOOD FRIENDS

11

Great friends, from left - Sylvia Hassenfeld, Bea Solomon, Barbara Levinson, Isabelle, Joy Wolf, and Phyllis Mailman (1997)

*A*s I write this history, I have been saddened by the news that Kitty Carlisle Hart has died. I first became acquainted with Kitty while she was chairman of the New York State Council on the Arts, a position she held under three different administrations. She was often in the governor's office, and we saw each other at various state events. She was also a close friend of Phyllis Cerf Wagner (she and Phyllis's deceased husband, Bennett Cerf, were celebrity panelists on the *What's My Line* television program), and was always at the parties I attended at the Wagners' home. We really became close while flying together on a business trip to Albany. She was appearing in a summer stock production that year and while en route she asked if I would cue her on her lines. I was happy to do so, but thought it very strange that everything she said sounded like real conversation and none of my lines sounded anything like that. It was during the exercise of going back and forth with her lines that I learned what it meant to be an actress—you had to put expression into the words you recited. Kitty continued to perform well into her nineties. It was fascinating that while she had to read all of her speaking lines, when it came to singing, she needed no help in remembering every word. Her memorial, several months after she died, was a sparkling celebration of her life. Dozens of Broadway stars saluted her, the Mayor and former Governor Cuomo spoke, and clips were shown from her early movies and TV shows. As Kitty would have wished, a good time was had by all.

Kitty Carlisle Hart, always the life of the party

Another great memory I have of Kitty is of a dinner party at Pauline Trigere's beautiful country home (Pauline, one of America's great couturiers, was addicted to turtles and in addition to naming her home in their honor, she had a

Good Friends

collection of hundreds of the tiny animals). That evening was extremely hot and the air conditioning was not working, so after dinner most of the guests were sitting outside chatting. After a few minutes, we noticed that the hostess and Kitty were not among us. Just about then, the two octogenarian women appeared, dressed in bathing suits, and off they went to take a swim. Kitty was famous for her beautiful legs and Pauline had a beautiful set to match. Over the years, I shared many lunches and dinners with both beauties, and they added much pleasure to my life.

On the occasion of Pauline's ninetieth birthday party, she reserved Le Grenouille restaurant and gave a dinner for ninety people. I asked if I could sit next to Senator Pat Moynihan, whom I had gotten to know quite well in the days when he was our ambassador to the UN, but she said no and wouldn't tell me why. The evening of the party, I discovered the reason; Pauline's table of ten consisted of the hostess and nine men, and she reserved the place at her right for the senator. She was a talented, dynamic, interesting, and amusing person, the ideal guest at any dinner party. Unfortunately, she too is gone.

As one grows older, especially when one is not married, a large group of friends is necessary in order to have a full life. I am fortunate to have had a wonderful coterie of people, many of whom I have already mentioned including Lorraine Silberthau, Sylvia Hassenfeld, Marifé Hernandez and Joel Bell, Audrey and Enriquillo del Rosario, Steve Stempler, Ruth and Leo Marks, Beverly Sills, and Jackie Loewe Fowler who I have known since my Wellesley days. But I would be remiss, indeed, if I did not mention some others. I have known Arlene Dahl and her husband, Marc Rosen, for thirty years and

Marc Rosen and Arlene Dahl

number them among my nearest and dearest. Arlene, of course, is the great movie beauty of the 1950s and 1960s, but she is so much more than that. She has been a successful businesswoman, an author, a horoscope expert, and a weekly columnist in that field. She is not only one of the most beautiful women in the world, but also one of the sweetest. I have never heard her say an unkind word about anyone. Marc is a creative businessman who has a flourishing design company. He and I are on the phone at least twice a week and exchange confidences regularly. He is a marvelous party planner and has organized successful events for the many causes he champions, as well as for many private occasions.

Joy and Erving Wolf and I began to develop a relationship when we joined the Palm Beach Country Club almost simultaneously. We also live in close proximity. They are ardent collectors of American furniture and art, which fill their magnificent New York apartment. Joy and I lunch together, giggle together, confide in each other, and give parties together. I often dine with them in New York and Palm Beach.

I must also mention Phyllis Mailman, who is one of the busiest women I know. She combines her ownership of a small clothing store and membership on the boards of Lincoln Center Theater and The Pierre hotel with her duties at the Mailman School of Public Health, which she established at Columbia University Medical Center. Then there is Russell Hemenway, who has been my good friend since 1972 when Claiborne Pell asked him to look after me, and he has done so all these years. Russ heads the National Committee for an Effective Congress and was one of the early presidents of the Lexington Democratic Club. He is an intelligent, handsome, debonair gentleman, and we have had lots of good times together.

Other close friends of mine are Jackie and Ira Neimark. I knew Jackie when she was (I thought) a young girl in Providence.

Jackie and Ira Neimark

It turns out we're the same age, but I already had children when we met and she was not yet married. We lost track for years, but after I returned to New York our paths crossed again since Ira was chairman of Bergdorf Goodman and we met on many social occasions. They also belong to Century Country Club and we see each other almost every weekend. Ira recently wrote a book, *Crossing Fifth Avenue to Bergdorf Goodman: An Insider's Account on the Rise of Luxury Retail*, for which I gave him a book party. The book has been very well received. He had so much fun doing it that it was one of the things that inspired me to sit down and write my own history.

My best golfing buddy at Century is Joan Tisch. I knew Joan's late husband, Bob, through my political work even before I met Joan. Bob was one of the nicest, most generous, and most popular men in New York City. Joan has the most marvelous sense of humor and continues to be one of our city's outstanding philanthropists. I really enjoy her company. Larry and Dalia Leeds were among the first couples I met after returning to New York, the introduction being made by my father. I spent many great weekends at their home in Stamford and it was there that I met many of the people who became my good friends at Century.

I had been friendly with Joy Israel for many years, and since her marriage to Harry Goldstein, we have become even closer. I was also close to Barbara and Tommy Hess for many years; Barbara and I spoke nearly every day. Unfortunately, she was one of my first pals to pass away. Several years later, Tommy married Peggy Hess and we too became good friends. Honey Wolosoff, Carmel Malkin, Sharon and Fred Klingenstein, and Harriette and Noel Levine are other friends with whom I have had many good times. And there are dozens more who have helped make my life in New York such a joy.

Some of those in Palm Beach with whom I golf, play bridge, have lunches, dinners, and parties are Helaine Allen, Judy Goldfarb, Gladys Benenson, Audrey Larman, Molly and Howard Weiss, Penny and Cecil Rudnick, Barbara Rackoff, Gigi Danziger, Annette Eskind, Betty Reitman, Helen and

Good Friends

Morty Sweig, Buddy Tamarkin, and Barbara Levinson who sadly passed away in January of 2008 after a long illness. Elliot Schnall is a long-time Palm Beacher whose company I enjoy because he is very bright and can always make me laugh. The first time I visited his home and saw a picture of his ex-wife, I realized that she and I had gone to Sunday school together. I find that in Palm Beach you meet up with people you have known in every other phase of your life—high school, college, travel, career, etc. Sometimes, it really does seem that there are only four hundred people in the world and they all know each other. All of these people have added immeasurably to the happy times I have found in Florida.

Celebrating with Lorraine

REFLECTIONS
12

People have often asked what made me become a Democrat. That is easy to answer; I learned it at my father's knee. He not only believed in the philosophy of the Democratic Party, he lived his life in accordance with its principles. When the war came and the owners of small stores had difficulty getting merchandise, he always remembered that they too had to make a living. The workers in his factories were treated so well that year after year they voted against having a union. I was brought up with no prejudice, only the understanding that the wondrous opportunities of this country should be available to every citizen. To me, it has always been obvious that the Democratic Party was the better vehicle for ensuring that those opportunities are provided, as exemplified by Democrats like Eleanor and Franklin Delano Roosevelt. At a dinner party I attended one evening, FDR's son, John, asked what led me into politics, and I replied, "It was my admiration for your father."

I have also been asked how I stood the ugliness of politics for so long. My answer has always been that it was not so ugly in the days that I was active. Most people went into the field with a desire to serve their country and solve its problems. Naturally, there were a few bad apples in the barrel, just as there are in finance, medicine, education, plumbing, engineering, and just about every human activity. But by and large, those in public office wanted to accomplish things, not merely secure power for its own sake. And while there was always partisanship, there was also a good deal of bipartisanship, particularly in foreign affairs. America was a different place in the mid-twentieth century and I feel fortunate to have participated in those good times.

Reflections

Although I have many wonderful friends, my family is, of course, my greatest source of pleasure. My sister Norma and my cousin Lorraine are very important in my life. My son and daughter, David and Amy, have showered me with love for all these many years, and although I am certain that there are many times when I annoy them, they keep coming back for more. As for my grandchildren, Nicky, Stephanie, Matthew, and Kelley, they are all bright and beautiful and give every evidence of being nearly as devoted to me as I am to them. Nicky is as sweet and good-hearted as his father. My only regret is that we live separated by an entire continent. Stephanie is a kind and dear person who genuinely cares about people. While she has a soft heart, she can be very determined about what she wants to accomplish and usually reaches her goals. She is a real beauty and not only did she inherit the family love of clothes, but she has her own unique and innate sense of style. Matthew is an unusual young man with an extraordinary interest and curiosity about everything. He is a voracious reader, an excellent writer, a fine musician, and combines an inner gentleness with his strength. Kelley is also extremely pretty, very sweet, quite artistic, and about to get married in the summer of 2008. All of them are the blessings of my life.

For my seventieth birthday, Amy had a marvelous faux Monopoly board made with all the important events of my life inscribed in the places that regularly appear on the board. It sits in a spot of honor in the garden room of my Greenwich home. For that birthday, the only celebration I wanted was a dinner with my immediate family, but by the time I reached eighty, I agreed to a larger celebration, and there were two events. Just before my birthday, my friends Sylvia, Marc and Arlene, and Marifé and Joel, gave me a fabulous soiree at Doubles in New York. There were about thirty people, all of whom I love, lots of gaiety, many toasts, a great dinner, and wonderful wine.

Reflections

For my actual birthday I was in Florida, and the children gave a dinner for our extended family, twenty-four in all. Unfortunately, the two major absences were my grandchildren, Stephanie and Matthew. They had exams at school and it was impossible for them to get away. This family gathering too was a splendid occasion. The children had written to all the guests and asked them to send old photos and to write something about me. Those efforts were assembled into a large album and to this day, each time I look at it my eyes fill with tears as I read the beautiful things that were written.

As I look back over my life, there are certain observations I would like to make. I have been extraordinarily lucky in having led a long life of good health, many interesting experiences, great luxury, and much love. Like everyone else, I have suffered periods of physical illness and emotional distress, but by and large, I have been a very happy person. Neither as a youth nor as an adult was I ever really an observant Jew, attending services only on the High Holidays, but I have always felt a deep cultural attachment to Judaism. It bothers me that my grandchildren probably do not have that same strong feeling, but I would hope that I have conveyed enough of my feeling to them that they will pass it on to their children. I do feel that is happening with my grandson Matthew. While most of my charitable endeavors have been to Jewish causes, as well as to educational institutions, hospitals, and health organizations, in some cases I have followed my father's example of giving anonymous gifts to various other charities. It is my fervent wish that my descendants will continue that pattern of giving. It is also my strong belief that there is nothing in life more important than one's family and I hope that my children, grandchildren, and great grandchildren will do everything possible to maintain close ties with their own families.

The world today is very different from the one that I have enjoyed for so long. It is a cause of great sorrow to me that I cannot bequeath that same kind of world to my descendants. I am gravely troubled about the heritage we are leaving for future generations. All of my friends agree that those years of our youth, just after World War II to the millennium, were the best of times—the "Greatest Generation," as Tom Brokaw noted in his recent book. Today, we are waging a war that we had no reason to start and even less reason to continue. We have allowed our freedoms to be eroded. We have ignored the environment for far too long and we have taken too few steps to rid our country of its dependence on foreign oil. We have lost the respect and admiration of the entire world. I fear that it will take a very long time to undo the harm that has been created in just the past seven years.

During the years of my adulthood, America was prosperous and the United States was respected by the entire world. Both our dollar and the products we manufactured were sought after. Our army was there to protect us should the need arise, but we felt totally safe within our own shores. Today, we are a debtor nation, we manufacture very little, and have become a service economy. Our army is stretched so thin that we are using our National Guard for overseas duty. Our homeland has been attacked and is vulnerable to further attack, and we are hated throughout most of the world. Although I have always been an optimist, it is very difficult for me to avoid being apprehensive about the future of my family and my country. I can only hope that you, my children and my grandchildren, will ponder these problems and do whatever you can to address them and seek the leadership for our country that will restore the damage that has been done over the last few years. Having said all this, I still firmly believe that there is no other country in the world that provides the freedom and opportunities that the United States does. I consider myself a genuine patriot, and I thank God every day that I am an American.

It is not enough to complain about the way things are, one must make an effort to correct things if even in a small way.

I'm not sure if was my father's influence, my Wellesley education, or a combination of the two, but through the years I have had an intense motivation to make a difference in the world in which I live. In striving towards that goal, sometimes I have succeeded and sometimes I have failed, but I have always focused my efforts in that direction. I hope that my descendents will inherit that same desire. To reinforce that commitment has really been the purpose of this remembrance. In a life full of pleasures, the writing of this history has been one of the most rewarding. It is my earnest hope that my children, grandchildren, and friends will enjoy reading it even half as much as I enjoyed writing it.

Early Family Photos

Facing page, clockwise from left: Grandfather David with his grandchildren. Standing from left are Irwin and Isabelle (note the glasses from the chicken pox episode). Seated from left are Lorraine and Norma.

Cousin Harold Gemeiner.

Grandmother Rebecca Aginsky Russack.

Grandfather Harry Bauman with Rose's cousin Esther Adler.

This page, clockwise from left: Cousin Lorraine.

Cousin Lorraine and Aunt Rose.

An early childhood photo, Isabelle & Norma.

David & Family

Clockwise from left: David, Amy and Nick; David enjoying the outdoors; Baby David; David, Kathy, and Marissa.

Amy & Family

Clockwise from left: Amy and Isabelle at Judy's wedding (1989); Amy and Baby Stephanie with Isabelle; the Brag Family (Anders, Steffi, Matthew, and Amy)

Good Friends

Clockwise from left: Sylvia Hassenfeld, Isabelle, and Phyllis Mailman at a party they cohosted; enjoying the company of Elliot Schnall; pals June Paley and Ruth Marks

A bridge game, from left: Isabelle, Susie Kornreich, Audrey Larman, Helaine Allen, and Sylvia Hassenfeld

Isabelle & Steve Stempler
(photo printed with permission of Lucien Capehart)

Isabelle, Jerry Tishman, and Marifé Hernandez
(photo printed with permission of Mort Kaye)

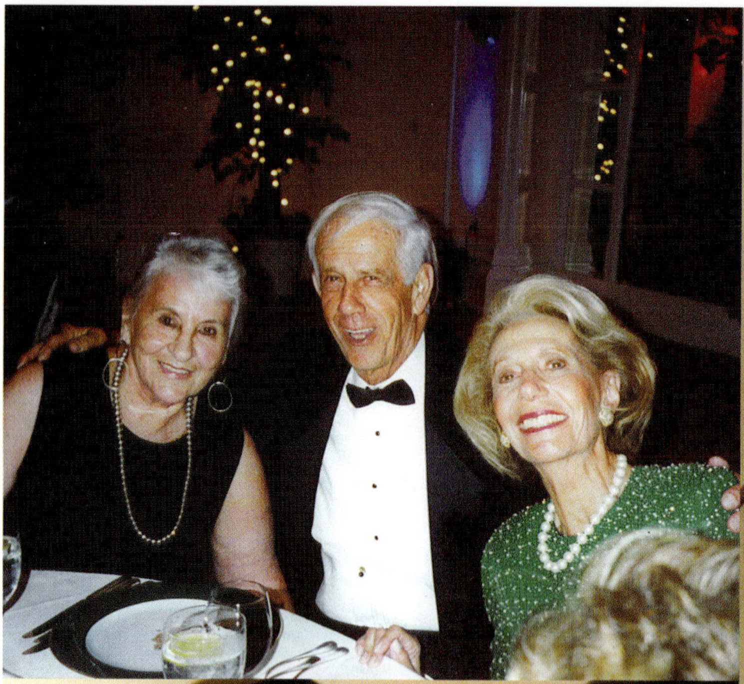
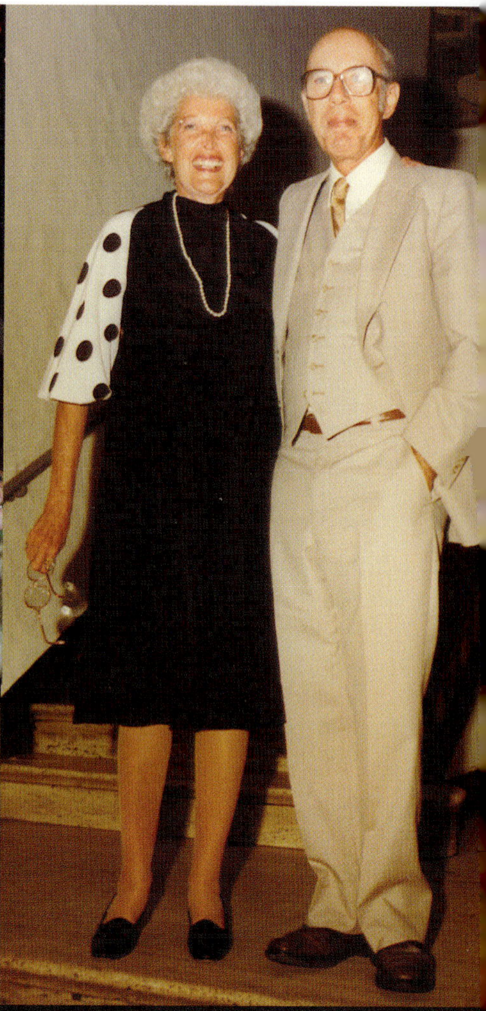
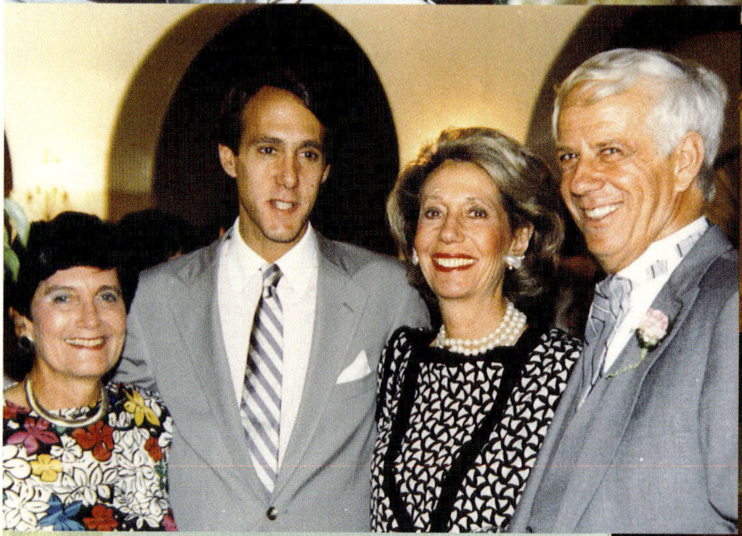
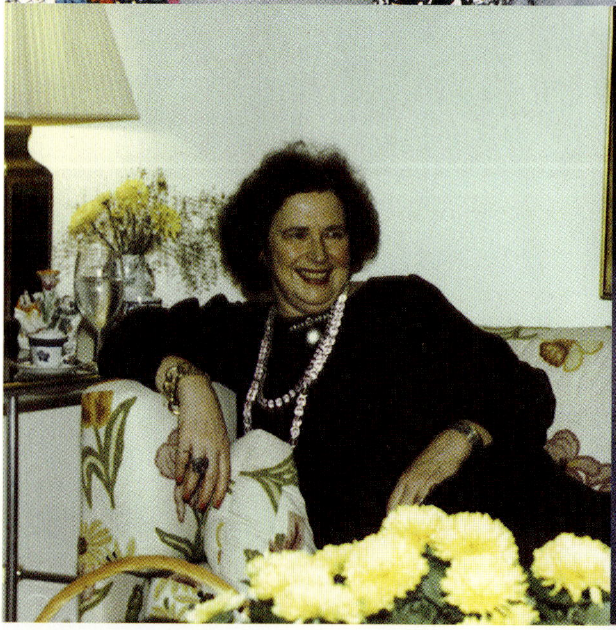
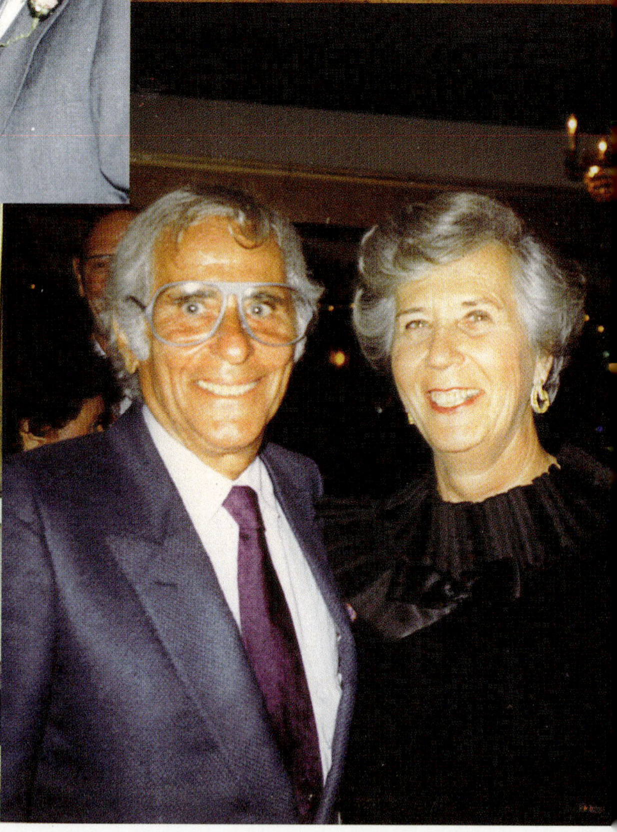

Family and Friends

With Norma in Palm Beach
(printed with permission of Mort Kaye)

Facing page, clockwise from top left: with cousin George Gemeiner and wife Muriel; Lorraine & Heinz Silberthau; my sister Norma and her husband Murray Grabler; my college pal Jackie Fowler; with David and cousins Bobbie Gemeiner and George Gemeiner

Grandchildren

A young Yankee fan - Nicky

Matthew and Stephanie (1992)

Matthew (1991)

Nick Steffi and Matthew (1992)

Steffi

Nick - cross country champ

Nick

Family and Grandchildren

Matthew and Stephanie

Stephanie's graduation from Brown University, 2008. Photo taken just after Isabelle had the privilege of handing Stephanie her diploma.

With David, Amy, Stephanie, and Matthew

Family Thanksgiving, clockwise from left: Anders; Isabelle's niece, Judy Jurney; David; Isabelle; Nick; Ruiz Jurney; Amy; Matthew; Stephanie; Judy and Ruiz's son, Ben

Family photo, from left: Matthew, Nick, Amy, David, Isabelle, Stephanie

Nick graduating from St. George's School

Isabelle's 80th Birthday Party

David, Marissa, Kathy, Nicholas, and Kelley

David, Isabelle, and Amy

Amy and Sidney Cooperman (cousin Lorraine's husband)